THE DYING DAYS OF SEGREGATION
IN AUSTRALIA:
CASE STUDY YARRABAH

By Barbara Miller 2018

2nd edition
Copyright © 2018 by Barbara Miller
Publisher Barbara Miller Books, PO Box 425 Westcourt, Cairns, 4870, Australia
B.A. (Hons) Psych, Grad Dip Sociology, MAPS, FDRP
The author may be contacted at www.barbara-miller-books.com

ISBN 978-0-9953691-6-0   eBook Kindle
ISBN 978-0-9953691-5-3   Paperback
ISBN 978-0-9953691-7-7   eBook Smashwords

This has been updated from a work originally published as *The aspirations of Aborigines living at Yarrabah in relation to local management and human rights* March 1986 for the Human Rights Commission as Discussion Paper No 7. The Human Rights Commission ceased to operate in mid-1986 and was replaced by the Human Rights and Equal Opportunities Commission.

Cover design by David Jack.
Front cover painting: *Dreams and Visions* by Munganbana Norman Miller.
Back cover map courtesy of Yarrabah Aboriginal Shire Council
http://www.indiginet.com.au/yarrabah

DOWNLOAD FREE GIFT NOW

Just to thank you for buying my book, I would like to give you a 14 page PDF of the hidden history of the first contact of Europeans with Australian Aborigines. It was at Mapoon. It is the untold story that is not in your school text books. Hear from Aborigines who have had the story passed down through generations and from the explorers.

For information on my other books go to – www.barbara-miller-books.com

TO DOWNLOAD GO TO
http://eepurl.com/dn69ab

Yarrabah Demonstration Against Proposed Closure of Aboriginal Communities in Western Australia.
Photo by Christine Howes 2015

Author at Guyala Lookout with Yarrabah houses below.
Photo by Norman Miller 2016

Former Yarrabah Chairman Roy Gray and his cousin Grace Ludwick at Roy's home.

Photo recent, private collection.

Courtesy Yarrabah Aboriginal Shire Council

Roy Gray, former Chairman of Yarrabah.

Courtesy Yarrabah Aboriginal Shire Council

Teachers Rev Les Baird back row 2nd from left and Rev Mick and
ValConnolly front row far right and middle with Wontulp Bi-Buya
students from the Kimberleys. Mick was Deputy Chairman of
Yarrabah in 1984.

Former Mayor of Yarrabah Percy Neal on Yarrabah Beach
Photo by Brendan Francis 2000 Newspix 15 Dec 2001

Bishop Bill Rays seated, Bishop Arthur Malcolm and tribal elders in coronation ceremony of King Vincent Jabaan Schreiber of Gunggandji tribe at Yarrabah

Photo Stewart McLean Newspix 10 Dec 2011

Yarrabah dancers with Parmunis Mundraby far left.

Private collection

Rico Noble, Yarrabah traditional owner, with author at Cairns NAIDOC Breakfast 2016. Rico's father Peter Noble and grandfather Mark Noble and the author were key figures in the original North Qld Land Council while Rico is a key figure in the current North Qld Land Council.

Photo by Norman Miller

Vince Mundraby, former Mayor of Yarrabah and former Chairperson Mandingalbay Yidinji Aboriginal Corporation.

Photo Djunbunji Ltd 2011

**Alf Neal key leader in Yarrabah and in
North Qld Land Council in 1970's and 1980's**
Photo at NAIDOC Ball Cairns 2017. Private collection

**Yarrabah Council at Parliament House Canberra 11 Sept 1979 L   R Stan
Connolly, Charlie Fourmile, Percy Neal (Chair) Romaine Yeatman,
Vince Schreiber (not in pic) and Shorty O'Neill, NQ Land Council.
Front, Robert Smallwood, The Canberra Times**

Mick Connolly, Deputy Chairman of Yarrabah in 1984
Courtesy Yarrabah Aboriginal Shire Council

Book Launch at Yarrabah author with Henrietta Fourmile Marrie Gimuy Walubarra Yidinji traditional owner and Rev Dorita Wilson who did the Welcome to Country 31 Oct 2016.
Photo Norman Miller

About the Author

B arbara Joyce Miller, historian, researcher and sociologist, co-founded, with her husband Norman, the Centre for International Reconciliation and Peace in 1996. She has been recognized by Worldwide Who's Who for showing dedication, leadership and excellence in humanitarian affairs. She lives in Cairns, Australia, with her husband Norman and son Michael.

Barbara is very passionate about Aboriginal advancement and liaises with religious and other communities worldwide through the Centre for International Reconciliation and Peace, which provides services focused on healing the wounds of history and reconciliation between people groups. With her husband, Norman, she pastors the Tabernacle of David congregation and she leads groups of Australians to Israel for Christian conferences and prayer tours. Barbara has forty years of professional experience not only in Aboriginal affairs, but also as a psychologist and mediator. She has her own business—Mediation Works Qld—and is an expert in mediating workplace and large-scale community disputes and family-law matters. Barbara is a motivated, inspiring teacher and counsellor who holds a postgraduate degree in sociology and a Bachelor of Arts with honours in psychology.

As a social justice campaigner, she helped the Mapoon people move back to their land. In the 90s, Barbara served as the CEO of the Aboriginal Coordinating Council through which she lobbied state and federal governments and wrote reports on topics such as native title, Indigenous resource management, local government, human rights, crime prevention in Aboriginal communities, health and deaths in custody. She has also authored various books and articles, including books titled *William Cooper, Gentle Warrior: Standing Up for Australian Aborigines and Persecuted Jews*, 2012, *The European Quest to Find Terra Australis Incognita: Quiros, Torres and Janszoon*, 2014, and *White Woman Black Heart: Journey Home to Old Mapoon, A Memoir* 2018.

Acknowledgements

I would like to acknowledge my faith in the God of Abraham, Isaac and Jacob and His Messiah. It is my Christian faith that has given me a strong social justice focus. I wrote this originally in 1984 when my son Michael Miller was five years old and I wrote it with the encouragement and support of my then husband, Mick Miller, who was Chairman of the North Queensland Land Council, an organization we established together. Mick's father, Mick Miller Snr, was sent to the penal colony of Palm Island off Townsville for punishment for speaking up for his rights. Mick's mother's father, George Sibley, was also sent to Palm Island for punishment, with his family, for being "cheeky", i.e. standing up for his rights. So Mick was born on Palm Island to Mick and Cissie Miller who met and married on Palm Island. I would like to honour their legacy. I would also like to thank the Aboriginal people of Yarrabah and Cairns for their contribution to this book and pioneering contribution to Aboriginal affairs.

In printing an updated second edition with a fresh title and cover, I want to thank my wonderful husband of twenty-five years, Norman Miller, for his belief in me and support. Norman's grandfather, Thomas Miller, was part of the stolen generation, taken from his mother at Nyleta when he was five years old. Norman's parents, Barclay and Shirley Miller have been a wonderful influence in my life. Barclay was part of the generation of Aboriginal people who were not allowed to be educated past Grade 4 so he was self-educated. Once he applied for a permit to go to Weipa South Aboriginal reserve (now Napranum) with his federal government job and was refused because they thought it was me. We had the same name—B. Miller.

I would like to thank Philip Newey for turning the first edition into an ebook and paperback and Will Silva for a wonderful job on the second edition. Thanks to David Jack for another amazing book cover and Munganbana's eye-catching painting on the front cover.

Thanks also to the present Yarrabah Aboriginal Shire Council led by Mayor Ross Andrews and Deputy Mayor Michael Sands for approval of the book and hosting the launch at Yarrabah on DOGIT Day 31 October 2016. DOGIT Day will be especially significant in 2016 as it is the thirtieth anniversary of the day Yarrabah received its deed of grant in trust (first land grant). It was delivered in person, said Mr Sands, by Queensland Minister for Aboriginal Affairs, Bob Katter, who arrived in a helicopter with lollies for the children.

Story of Cover Painting—Dreams and Visions
By Munganbana Norman Miller

Limited Edition Lino Print
150 x 150mm

This black and white print shows me thinking, dreaming, imagining, looking at the possibilities before me. I am musing, creating what might be. It is as if the circles are bubbles of thought and above them to the top left there are rivers of possibilities, stepping stones to the fulfilment of my dreams. On the right are vine leaves I can climb up into the future, the rainforest holding its treasures for me to find.

Endorsements

I have known Barbara Miller since the early 1990s when she was the Chief Executive Officer for Aboriginal Coordinating Council that was the peak body established by the Queensland Government to represent fourteen Aboriginal local government councils in Queensland.

Barbara has always had a keen unrelenting interest in social justice and community development of Aboriginal people stemming back from the 1970s and when I met her in the 1990s her dedication to the advancement of Indigenous Affairs has never ceased to amaze me.

Barbara has published four books and written several journal articles and I respect the excellent qualities of her work. This book is of significant historical value not only for Yarrabah but Aboriginal people across the country can relate to it through their own stories. I strongly recommend this book *The Dying Days of Segregation in Australia: Case Study Yarrabah*. I can testify that I have lived in this era, when segregation was in its dying days.

Reflecting on my own experience of segregation in Broome as a boy in the 1960s, I recall waiting with the patients of the 'Native' Hospital for the doctor to finish attending to his white patients first.

And another time enjoying a movie at the Sun Picture Theatre meant finding seating on the hard wooden seats at the back of the room, not the comfortable 'white only' canvas seats at the front. I used to sit on those hard wooden chairs.

Thankfully, times were changing. When I came to live in Yarrabah in 1984, the days of the white only section and black only sections in the town, drawn up by the Department of Native Affairs, was coming to an end. As we watched them begin to let go of their power and control of our lives, this made me feel good. Like Barbara, I have been active in our people's movement to control our own local government affairs to this day.

Les Baird, Temporary Training Co-ordinator, Wontulp-Bi-Buya College 2006–2016, Health Manager Gurriny Yealamucka Health Service, Yarrabah 2000–2005.

There remains a current and deliberate national void in how Australia has and continues to treat Aboriginal peoples. The rule of law is further away than before because of native title; the legal concept that Aboriginal peoples still own land. The Yarrabah mission was one of the first to have its Aboriginal hostages aired in the Australian High Court in *Neal v R 149 CLR 305* (the spitting case). Yarrabah was one of the many Aboriginal missions in Queensland set apart from public view where the white manager held unaccountable powers over Aboriginal life and death in the community. On a click of his fingers Aboriginal families could be torn apart and removed from the community.

This why Barbara Miller's book *The Dying Days of Segregation in Australia: Case Study Yarrabah* remains so important. Why were Aboriginal peoples subjected to living under constant threats and more importantly, why did the rest of the country take no interest and do nothing? It was Barbara Miller that exposed all this and lessons are still unfolding or ignored from what she wrote then as the same mistakes are being repeated. This book should be a standard school text book.

George Villafor, CEO of first Cape York Peninsula Aboriginal legal service, current CEO of Ngambri Local Aboriginal Land Council, Queanbeyan, NSW.

It is entirely appropriate that Barbara Miller is the one to write an update on Yarrabah's efforts at self-determination and land rights, as she does not just stand on the sideline and cheer us on. She often jumps into the fray herself. No doubt many people who were or still are involved in some degree in the push for Aboriginal social justice and human rights and all that that encompasses, plus interested persons, will be attracted to Barbara Miller's latest case study. This book gives a succinct report of how things have turned out in the last thirty years. She has ably teased out the many strands of human rights issues that reveal the many flash points that happened as Aboriginal people and friends contended with, and still contend with the 'hydra-like monster'. Her reporting skills and love for Aboriginal people are recognised by friend and foe alike, with her work being quoted by such bodies as the Human Rights Commission.

Rev Michael Connolly, Former Chairman of Yarrabah, August 2016.

This is an excellent coverage of the milestones in the contemporary historical coverage of our Indigenous Queenslander's struggle for Land Rights and freedom from the autocratic control of Government. It is works such as this that clearly identify the oppressive control and heinous actions of the Department of Aboriginal and Islander Advancement. The hypocrisy of including 'Advancement' in their name, when they did the exact opposite, only underlines the Machiavellian treatment of Queensland's First Nation people. Miller has clearly and effectively covered the momentous changes that have been wrought. Only someone who has lived and worked with these trials and tribulations could explain the events so well. This is undoubtedly a valuable contribution to understanding the hard-fought steps that our Indigenous people have had to overcome, and it's not over—but now there is room for hope!

Dr Timothy Bottoms, historian, author of *Conspiracy of Silence and a History of Cairns, City of the South Pacific 1770–1995*. August 2016.

All of the facts that Barbara Miller writes about have brought many positive changes. As a seventy-one-year-old survivor of the Yarrabah experiences, I am now finding peace for myself by reflecting on the errors of the past. We all learn in our human spirit to not allow ourselves to be governed by other hurtful narcissist human beings.

Roy Gray, former Chairman Aboriginal Coordinating Council, former Chairman of Yarrabah and former Manager Menmuny Museum Yarrabah. August 2016.

This important book documents the vicissitudes and challenges of Yarrabah, Queensland's largest Deed of Grant in Trust (DOGIT) Aboriginal community ... [I]n a rapidly changing mainstream political landscape and with no constitutional protections, the people of Yarrabah face an uncertain future. An uncertain future which includes legislative insecurity which could see Yarrabah lands parcelled up as freehold and lost to outside developers eager to get their hands on Yarrabah's billion-dollar coastal real estate, potential amalgamation with the Cairns Regional Council, and loss of community agency as community-based service provision falls victim to the 'Indigenous industry' populated by those who make a living from Aboriginal misery. For the sake of its youthful population, Yarrabah today must find a way to take back control of its destiny and reassert itself through its leadership as a viable and vigorous Aboriginal community, protecting its identity and culture while participating in and contributing to the greater Australian society. By shining a light on the political and policy landscape of the last forty years that has shaped the Yarrabah of today, this book offers much to ponder when considering Yarrabah's prospects for the future—a future that all of Queensland's DOGIT communities must, in their own way, contemplate going forward.

Henrietta Marrie, Associate Professor, Office of Indigenous Engagement CQUniversity Cairns, August 2016.

FOREWORD

I t was a wonderful privilege to be able to research and write this book as the leaders and people of Yarrabah Aboriginal community near Cairns took me into their hearts and confidence to share the pain of the past and their hopes for the future.

I was able to write it at incredible timing—on the cusp of the change from the discriminatory Queensland Aborigines Act 1971–79 to the Community Services (Aborigines) Act 1984 which gave elected Aboriginal councils limited freedom to run their communities. For nearly 100 years, i.e. since 1897, Aborigines had been living under oppressive legislation designed originally to protect them from the ravages of white society including outright slaughter, poisoning of flour and waterholes, kidnapping to work on ships, child labour etc. The Aboriginals Protection and Restriction of the Sale of Opium Act 1897, which continued through some changes and in 1984 was the Queensland Aborigines Act, allowed Aborigines to be rounded up, put on reserves, and live under segregation similar to the apartheid regime in South Africa with its permit system.

Although the Racial Discrimination Act 1975 was enacted by the Australian Government, the Queensland Government refused to comply with Australia's international human rights commitments and the federal legislation. Finally in 1984, the Queensland Government passed the Community Services (Aborigines) Act which gave a measure of local government to Aboriginal reserves who were thereafter called communities. Amendments were made to the Land Act so that the Aboriginal councils could hold the land in trust for the communities giving communal ownership. This was a big step forward as well though it fell short of land rights legislation that was finally enacted in Queensland in 1991 and the native title legislation enacted federally in 1993 after the Mabo decision.

Previous to the Land Act (Aboriginal and Islander Land Grants) Amendment Act 1984 or (DOGIT), which is examined in detail in this book, Aborigines were not allowed to own land in Queensland as the reserves were considered crown land. The human rights infringements of the outgoing and incoming legislation in 1984 was examined and the horrifying situation of Queensland Aboriginal communities exposed.

So at Yarrabah, and for Queensland former Aboriginal reserves, 1984 was a life-changing moment. That's why this book is so important. So hot was it at the time that the Human Rights Commission, for which it was originally written, did not publish it until March 1986, just before they wound up. It was too controversial to federal-state politics to release it sooner. The Commission did use my paper to prepare its own report on the Community Services (Aborigines) Act (Report No. 9).

However, I do not leave it there. The last chapter, 'Thirty Years On', covers the changes nationally and in Yarrabah over the last thirty years that have led to the situation today re segregation, local or self-government, land rights and native title. I think it is particularly interesting that Chairman of the Yarrabah Council, Percy Neal, was progressing a native title test case for Yarrabah concurrently with the Mabo case until the Queensland Government targeted him and he was jailed for two months after confronting the white store manager and asking him to leave the community. The names Neal and Yarrabah could have been as well known as Mabo and Murray Island (Mer).

Yarrabah Trust Areas

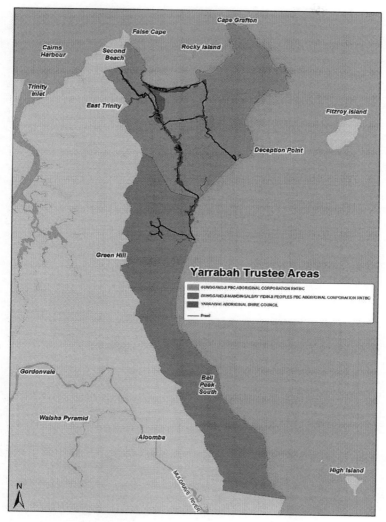

Map provided by Yarrabah Aboriginal Shire Council.

CONTENTS

xix

THIRTY YEARS ON

T he research I did in Yarrabah, hearing the voices and hearts of Aboriginal people there in 1984 re governance, land rights and human rights was published in 1986. So this chapter answers the question 'What is the current situation?' and the question 'What's happened in the last thirty years?'

Orwellian Control and Critical Time of Writing

Orwell's book *1984* introduced the term 'Big Brother' for the kind of control and scrutiny the government held over the lives of people in his novel. It is striking that in Queensland, it is 1984 when this kind of Orwellian Big Brother relationship of the state to Indigenous people came to an end with the abolition of the Queensland Aborigines Act and its counterpart, the Torres Strait Islanders Act. 'The Acts' had existed for nearly ninety years. I should say segregation legally came to an end as it dragged on for a few more years as this book will show. I cannot overstate, however, the turning point that occurred in 1984, which is why, I believe, this book is so important.

It is written, primarily, at a time when one era came to an end and another era began and we see the emergence of a measure of local government and a measure of land ownership on Aboriginal and Torres Strait Islander communities in Queensland. We also see the gradual whittling away of human rights abuses. My writing was so hot and controversial at the time that it was not published until 1986 lest it raise the ire of the Queensland Government.

Segregation and Queensland Aborigines Act

Hence the title *The Dying Days of Segregation in Australia: Case Study Yarrabah*. Where does segregation come into it? Aboriginal people in Queensland (and other parts of Australia) were removed, often forcibly, from their tribal land and sometimes from their families, and moved onto government reserves or church missions. This was ostensibly to protect them from predatory European settlers but it also removed them out of the way of 'progress' so that the settler state could expand. The reserves and missions were administered under draconian Queensland Government legislation, known by Aboriginal people simply as 'the Act.'

Aboriginal people on reserves became wards of the state and adults were treated like children. Children were separated from their parents into boys' and girls' dormitories and were forbidden to speak their language and practice their culture. Aborigines had to have permits to live on or leave reserves, to visit reserves, to work off reserves, to marry etc. and the white manager had complete control over their lives. They could be removed from one reserve and sent to another at the whim of the government. Some reserves were run by the bell and had curfews and there were white sections and Aboriginal sections. When they did work off reserves in the white community, they did not receive their pay as the police or manager in control kept their bankbooks and doled them out some money, the bulk of it going into the government's Aborigines Welfare Fund which could be spent anywhere. Intergenerational poverty occurred because they were not allowed to buy houses or other assets or save money which could be passed on as an inheritance. The regulations to the Act even required Indigenous people to ask permission to use certain items of electrical equipment. It was possible to apply for exemption from the Act but it often meant not being able to visit family, community and land.

Les Malezer, currently the co-chair of the National Congress of First Nations, said in 2005 that Queensland, under Premier Joh

Bjelke-Petersen, was running an apartheid-like regime in the 1960s and 1970s:

> The laws that had been thrown out of the other states in the late 1960s were still operating in Queensland right up until the 1980s because Bjelke-Petersen refused to remove them. The racism in Queensland was regimented and institutionalised, and it lasted much longer than in other States—and it was an apartheid system ... From 1972 onwards, through both the Whitlam and then Fraser years, the federal government was constantly trying to override the Queensland government's 'Black Acts' in order to give Queensland Aboriginal people some sort of recognition and rights as people, but the Bjelke-Petersen government was fighting them on every turn.[1]

The same article said, 'In 1971 the World Council of Churches labelled the Queensland government's Aborigines Act "almost as iniquitous as South Africa's Apartheid'.

Did South Africa learn from Australia?

I have heard a number of Aboriginal people in Queensland claim that South Africa got its idea for the apartheid system from Australia. Mick Miller, chairman of the North Queensland Land Council, was one of these. Without researching government records from Queensland and South Africa on this issue, there is only anecdotal support for this contention. Apartheid is an Afrikaans word meaning apartness or separateness and describes a situation where a racial minority is forcefully segregated and experiences discrimination on many levels including legal discrimination. Apartheid was in force in South Africa from 1948 to 1994.

---

[1] 'Queensland's Darkest Days' *The Guardian* 8 June 2005.

Considering the White Australia Policy to keep non-Europeans out was established in 1901 and legislation based on protection and segregation of Aborigines was instituted in all states except Tasmania, which banished Aborigines to Cape Barron Island, one could see why it might appear that South Africa drew from Australia's experience. Colin Graham and Dr Trevor Cook are cited as maintaining that South Africa sent their experts to North Queensland to study the Aboriginals Protection and Restriction of the Sale of Opium Act 1897 (Qld) and took it back to implement.[2]

Town Camps and Curfews for Aborigines

Reserves often had black and white sections, like Palm Island and Yarrabah, for example. Segregation was not confined to keeping Aboriginal people on reserves or blacks and whites on reserves separate. A lot of Aboriginal people lived in camps on the fringes of towns without electricity and with only communal taps. Some Aboriginal people still live in town camps in, e.g., Alice Springs. Some cities and towns had a black line or boundary like Boundary Street in West End in Brisbane and Aboriginal people were prevented from being inside the city boundary after curfew. A letter to the editor from Toowong in *The Brisbane Courier* Monday 3 May 1875 says:

> They are not permitted to remain within the municipal boundaries after dark; but in order to enforce this regulation they are driven out at the point of the whip by mounted troopers. This process is anything but an elevating sight, reminding the onlooker more of the hunting of vermin than of the enforcement of law against human beings; and the way in which blackfellows, gins, and picaninnies will take to the

---

[2] 'Do We Have Apartheid in Australia?' by Jens Korff 2016, https://www.creativespirits.info/aboriginalculture/politics/do-we-have-apartheid-in-australia

water when too hard pressed by the horses, makes the vermin comparison still stronger.

In country towns in various parts of Australia, there was still segregation in the 1960s. This meant segregated school buses, hospitals, cinemas, and cemeteries. Aborigines were not allowed at all in RSL clubs even when they were ex-servicemen. They were not allowed in bowling clubs, swimming pools, town halls, shopping centres, pubs, hotels and football ovals. If they were served in shops, it was always last. Even on Thursday Island in the Torres Strait, there was a section for Indigenous people in the picture theatre and a section for non-Indigenous which was of a better standard.

Freedom Ride 1965

The freedom rides in the USA to break the colour bar inspired Aboriginal university student Charlie Perkins to lead a group of Sydney university students in a freedom ride through some New South Wales country towns in 1965. They were to experience angry resistance but did eventually bring gradual change and educated people in the process. Last year, some of those on the bus in 1965 reboarded the bus fifty years on to repeat the journey. Ann Curthoys recalls the 1965 trip.

'The first time we took children to the pool, there were a lot of arguments between us and the pool manager', says Professor Curthoys. After negotiating with the town's mayor, Professor Curthoys said they left Moree on the understanding the pool would be desegregated. Several days later, the bus would return to Moree, though, having found that the decision had been reversed. 'We came back and the second time was when the really fierce demonstration happened', she said. 'Eventually we were escorted out of there.' She said the reaction of those who protested against desegregation was horrifying. 'The threat of violence was there and I think that demonstrated just how fiercely people were going to defend their rights to segregation, and what you might call white supremacy', she says.[3]

Northern Territory Intervention

The Northern Territory Intervention, or Northern Territory National Emergency Response Act 2007, was the response of the federal government to the Northern Territory (NT) Government's Inquiry into the Protection of Aboriginal Children from Sexual Abuse, or 'Little Children are Sacred' report. The legislation received bipartisan support in the Commonwealth Parliament. Aboriginal people in the NT were excluded from the 1975 Racial Discrimination Act so the Commonwealth Government could make laws or 'special measures' that discriminated against them. The main initiative, Operation Outreach, was conducted by a force of 600 soldiers and concluded on 21 October 2008. Not one prosecution for child abuse has resulted. Despite this heavy-handed response to which many Aboriginal people objected, only two out of ninety-seven of the 'Little Children are Sacred' report's recommendations have been implemented. The Emergency Response has since been replaced by the very similar Stronger Futures Policy.

Seven-headed Monster

As I write this section to update my work written in May 1984, I start to write that segregation died a hard death in Australia, particularly in Queensland where Yarrabah is situated. Then I see it as a snake and its head being chopped off but it struggles and somehow survives and just won't die. Then I see it has many heads. The thought of a seven-headed monster comes to me—the hydra. Somehow it's

---

[3] 'Reboarding the Freedom Ride bus, 50 years on' by Jeremy Story Carter 20 February 2015 http://www.abc.net.au/radionational/programs/rnafternoons/freedom-ride-50-years-on/6163446

almost dead but the attitudes that feed it, keep it from dying completely.

What feeds segregation? What feeds apartheid? What was feeding this monster? Some of the drivers are fear of difference, greed for Aboriginal land, feelings of superiority and the belief that Aboriginal people weren't really human or were down the evolutionary chain. After all, it was not till 1973 that the final vestiges of the White Australia Policy were removed. Until 1967, Aborigines were not counted in the census as people but, incredibly, as fauna and flora, i.e. animals and plants. This is in living memory.

There were a number of times the axe chopped off the head of this seven-headed monster. Aboriginal people received voting rights in the 1960s, more than sixty years after being left out of the founding document or birth certificate of the nation, the Australian Constitution. The Yirrkala Bark Petition by the Yolngu in August 1963 protested the removal of over 300 km² from Arnhem land reserve for bauxite mining. It did not succeed but it weakened the monster as these are the first documents bridging Australian law and Indigenous law because the paintings depicted that law on bark and it was typed in English and Gumatj. It amounted to a documentary recognition of Indigenous people in Australian law as it conformed also to the protocols the parliament required of petitions.[4]

Another blow to segregation was the walk-off from Wave Hill Station by the Gurindji in August 1966 over low wages, poor working conditions and land rights, the latter being famously received in 1975 when Prime Minister Gough Whitlam poured soil in the hands of Gurindji leader Vincent Lingiari. We have just celebrated the fiftieth anniversary of what has been hailed as the birth of land rights though concerns at employment conditions there were still expressed.

In the 1967 referendum, a majority of Australians agreed to constitutional change so that Indigenous people should be counted in

---

[4] Yirrkala Bark Petitions 1963 (Cth) *Documentary a Democracy* http://www.foundingdocs.gov.au/item-did-104.html.

the census as people not as fauna and flora. No longer one dingo, one kangaroo, one palm tree, one wattle. They also agreed that the Commonwealth Government should be able to make laws for Indigenous people and the Commonwealth passed the Racial Discrimination Act 1975. Another chop at head of the segregation monster. The Queensland Government was in breach of this with its Queensland Aborigines Act. But it wouldn't budge. It didn't want to relinquish control of Indigenous people in its boundaries.

Assimilation

Most writers say that the government moved through the following stages in its policy re Indigenous people—protection and segregation and then assimilation and then self-management and self-determination. The Protection and Segregation era in Queensland is seen to be 1897–1965, Assimilation 1965–1984 and Self-Management after the Whitlam federal government came to power in the 1970s. Lately it is considered the Partnership era started in 2000. However, policies of segregation and assimilation were also occurring at the same time. From 1965 onwards, there was still strict control and legislative guardianship over the lives of Aborigines co-existing with the intent to transition them to mainstream society.

The most notable example of the assimilation policy was what has been termed as 'the Stolen Generation' where Aboriginal children were removed from their families and communities for having Aboriginal mothers and white fathers. They were put in institutions like boys' or girls' homes or missions and trained to fit into white society. Girls were sent out to work as domestic servants for negligible wages. They were only allowed to marry white or fairer Aborigines so that their Aboriginality would be bred out. This is covered in the Bringing Them Home Report of 1997 and the Rudd federal government and Nelson opposition gave a ground-breaking bipartisan apology in 2008. As this was an important symbolic gesture, the practical reconciliation measure of the Closing the Gap strategy was instituted by Prime Minister Kevin Rudd to lessen the wide disparity in socio-economic indicators between Indigenous and non-Indigenous Australians. More blows to the head of the segregation monster.

Self-Management and Self-determination

With the Yirrkala bark petition (1963) and the Wave Hill walk-off (1966), pressure was mounting for Aboriginal land rights. South Australia set up the Aboriginal Lands Trust in 1966. The Whitlam government introduced a policy of self-management in the 1970s but still the Queensland Government held out. Another chop, another blow. But the monster was not going to give up that easily. Whitlam set up the Aboriginal Land Rights Commission known as Woodward Royal Commission. In 1973, it recommended setting up the Northern and Central Land Councils in the Northern Territory (NT), the first government-recognised and funded land councils in Australia. In 1974 it recommended land rights legislation for the NT. It was before the parliament when the Whitlam government was dismissed by the Governor-General in November 1975. The Liberal government of Prime Minister Malcolm Fraser which followed passed a watered-down version—the Aboriginal Land Rights (Northern Territory) Act (Cwth) 1976 but it was still a historic moment. Another blow to the head.

The Springbok demonstrations in Queensland against apartheid in South Africa in 1971, the Aboriginal embassy demonstrations in Canberra in 1972, the North Queensland Land Rights Committee (1975), the North Queensland Land Council (1977) which campaigned nationally and internationally and the demonstrations against the Commonwealth Games in Brisbane in 1982 meant—chop, chop, chop, chop. The heads grew back but they were weakened. Yarrabah leaders who were significant in working for land rights through the North Queensland Land Council were Alf Neal, Mark Noble, Stan Connolly and Fred Mundraby.

There were a number of Indigenous organisations that effectively campaigned to abolish the Queensland Act. Among these were the Cairns Aboriginal and Torres Strait Islander Advancement League with Joe McGinness and Gladys O'Shane, the Federal Council for the Advancement of Aborigines and Torres Strait Islanders (FCAATSI), Brisbane Tribal Council, the Black Resource Centre with Cheryl Buchanan, the Foundation for Aboriginal and Islander Research Action (FAIRA) with Bob Weatherall and Les Malezer and Aboriginal Legal Services. FAIRA held a Two Laws conference in Brisbane in 1990 and, together with the Aboriginal Legal Service in Brisbane, did a survey of community attitudes which resulted in a publication *Beyond the Act* 1979 which is discussed in this book. Aboriginal Bill Rosser's book *This is Palm Island* 1978 also got the distressing information out about life under the Act. Fr Frank Brennan and the Catholic Bishops provided valuable legislative analysis and advocacy. Segregation was almost dealt a death blow with these actions.

The Discriminatory Qld (Aborigines) Act is Abolished

Then the Human Rights Commission asked me to report on the aspirations of Aborigines at Yarrabah re local government and human rights. After eighty-seven years of tyranny, subjugation and intimidation of Indigenous people in Queensland, from 1897 to 1984, the Queensland Government was finally putting to bed 'the Act'. Would it mean freedom? Would it mean self-management? Would it mean local government? Would it mean their human rights being respected?

The view of Yarrabah, which had been established as an Anglican mission in 1892 and became a government reserve in 1960, was no. It was just a name change. They had grave worries about it as you can see from the rest of my book. Aboriginal councils had an advisory role to government from 1960 to 1984 and now they were meant to be governing their own communities. The state government, however, still had a great deal of control but they were meant to phase themselves out in three years. For most of this time there were two administrations, the council and the government but the government held the purse strings. In 1986, the government did hand over to the Aboriginal council but the legislation was different to the local government legislation that non-Indigenous councils operated under.

These changes occurred grudgingly with great resistance from the Queensland Government who were responding belatedly to local, national and international pressure. Yarrabah was a vocal proponent of this change as can be seen from earlier chapters in this book. It was not that the Queensland Government had had a change of heart or had a fresh policy vision.

Award wages were finally paid to Aborigines at Yarrabah in 1986 after much lobbying by Arnold Murgha, who took an award wages test case, and lobbying by the North Queensland Land Council and Australian Workers Union. Stolen wages from Aboriginal workers in Queensland, which were paid into the Aborigines Welfare Fund, have never been returned. Reparations to a limit of $7,000 a person were

11

eventually paid between 2002 and 2010 if Aborigines could prove who they worked for and when, which was very difficult. Many had already died before receiving it. Remaining monies are in a trust fund to assist in the education of young Indigenous people in Queensland.

Mick Connolly, chairperson of Yarrabah Aboriginal Council, said on 16 May 1989, five years after the writing of the first edition of this book:

> The Council may have been a 'rubber stamp' in earlier years but by 1985 we had an independent attitude and were asserting our determination to self-manage. I now consider that we are three-quarters of the way along the path to self-management. If we had control of the funding, we would be there. We are seeking more power. The goal is to determine our own future.

The new Goss Labor government quickly set up the Legislative Review Committee to review management of Indigenous communities. Chaired by Mr Eric Deeral from Hopevale, the committee consisted of five Aborigines and Torres Strait Islanders. Their report was called the *Inquiry into the legislation relating to the management of Aboriginal and Torres Strait Islander communities in Queensland*. The Community Services legislation was amended to withdraw the paternalistic accounting and auditing procedures of Indigenous councils. The huge investigative power of visiting justices was repealed and, instead, provision was made for a magistrate to review the records of an Aboriginal court and to advise on appropriate sentencing. A sweeping change was that executive officers (in a similar role to white managers) were withdrawn from Aboriginal communities by October 1990 except in the Northern Peninsula Area which took a bit longer.

Government departments continued to manage many of the services delivered to Yarrabah into the 1990s and many council staff continued to be non-Indigenous. Gradually there was devolution of planning and program delivery to the local level in communities like Yarrabah with responsibility going to council or other organisations. Yarrabah and other Aboriginal councils were able to apply for grants, run services and employ more local people but capacity building became an issue with the new responsibilities.

Local Government Mainstreamed in 2004

A seismic shift gradually occurred. It took till 2004 for the Local Government (Community Government Areas) Act (Qld) to be passed and Aboriginal community councils became Aboriginal shires and the chairpersons became mayors. This included not only the communities like Yarrabah which had been under the Community Services Act (CSA) but also Aurukun and Mornington Island who were under different local government legislation as a result of a Queensland Government takeover of the reserve from the Presbyterian church in 1978. So now fourteen Aboriginal councils in Queensland had similar status to non-Indigenous councils, i.e. they were mainstreamed.

The Community Governance Improvement Strategy (CGIS) was a major initiative under the Queensland Government's Meeting Challenges, Making Choices strategy administered by the Department of Aboriginal and Torres Strait Islander Policy (DATSIP) to build capacity during a transition period over four years to the Local Government Act 1993. The government realised, however, that its past mistreatment of Indigenous people had led to distrust and cynicism re its motives:

> As a result of the past practices and policies outlined above, many Aboriginal and Torres Strait Islander people have limited trust or confidence in government engagement processes. Cynicism, fear and, at times, disbelief that

government is seeking the opinion of community members can all impact on engagement outcomes.[5]

The Council of Australian Governments (COAG) committed all Australian governments to a policy approach of partnerships and shared responsibility with Aboriginal and Torres Strait Islander people. This has meant mainstreaming of services and, in Queensland, the role of the Office for Aboriginal and Torres Strait Islander Partnerships changed from direct service delivery to policy development and coordination of other agencies.

Queensland developed a new framework of Ten Year Partnerships 2000–2010 with Aboriginal and Torres Strait Islander communities where government departments would sit down at negotiation tables with Indigenous councils and work out community development plans rather than just administer grants. The government, after community consultation, identified key areas for the Ten Year Partnership—justice, family violence, reconciliation, economic development, community governance, service delivery, human services, and land, heritage and natural resources.

Yarrabah Council

Mayor Vince Mundraby said:

> The former Yarrabah Community Council became the Yarrabah Aboriginal Shire Council on the 1 January 2005. The change to this legislation will create many challenges for the Yarrabah Community over the next year but will bring with it many opportunities that could benefit the community, such as processes that would be fair, transparent and equitable, identified career paths, business opportunities and a

---

[5] Qld Government 'Setting the Context' http://www.qld.gov.au/web/community-engagement/guides-factsheets/atsi-communities/setting-context.html.

sustainable future … During this year, we have already seen the emergence of new buzz words about Indigenous service delivery, 'mutual obligation' and 'shared responsibility'. The Commonwealth Government has created "Shared Responsibility Agreements" (SRAs) to give expression to this philosophy.[6]

Yarrabah Council employed around 200 people in 2004–5 and were responsible for 800 staff on the Community Development Employment Program (CDEP) or work for the dole. In July 2004, Aboriginal councils like Yarrabah were now serviced by Department of Local Government, Planning, Sport and Recreation not DATSIP.

Yarrabah Council has pursued its self-management policy by (a) achieving mainstream standards for councils in being fair, efficient and financially accountable; (b) building local capacity through training local staff which leads to staff stability and role models for youth; (c) good governance with councillors making policies and leaving operational matters to staff; and (d) partnerships with and engaging with government including other councils like Cairns City Council. Yarrabah Council negotiates with funding providers rather than just accepting the terms offered. For example, it promotes local people being employed instead of outside contractors on housing renovations. As Yarrabah is close to Cairns, the council and people have more exposure to the outside world than a lot of other Indigenous communities in Queensland and this may be a factor in the stronger engagement strategy the Yarrabah Council pursues.

Such has been Yarrabah's success that it was shortlisted in 2006 as one of eight national finalists in the Indigenous Governance Awards hosted by Reconciliation Australia and BHP Billiton.

---

[6] Yarrabah Shire Council *Annual Report 2004–*5 http://yarrabah.qld.gov.au/wp-content/uploads/2015/04/Annual-Report-2004-05-Part-One.pdf.

From Aboriginal Coordinating Council to Indigenous Leaders Forum

The Aboriginal Advisory Council, which represented Aboriginal councils on reserves, was disbanded and the Aboriginal Coordinating Council (ACC) was set up by the 1984 CSA Act with Eric Deeral as the first chairman. There were Torres Strait Islander counterparts. The ACC was given statutory powers to advise the government and consisted of the chairman and another councillor from each ex-reserve community. This was disbanded in 2004 as well by the mainstreaming process so that Indigenous councils became part of the Local Government Association of Queensland (LGAQ).

The Indigenous Leaders Forum (ILF) is a gathering of the leaders (mayors, councillors and CEOs) from the sixteen Queensland Aboriginal or Torres Strait Islander Queensland local government councils and also Torres Shire Council. The ILF is convened formally twice a year but occasionally will be brought together for specific-issue meetings as needed. The ILF was established by the LGAQ at the request of its Aboriginal and Torres Strait Islander Council members with relevant government ministers attending depending on the issues discussed.

A Cape Indigenous Mayors Alliance (CIMRA) was formed in 2013 and represents eight Aboriginal councils in Cape York but this does not include Yarrabah as it is near Cairns. It does include the Torres Shire Council and its purpose is to be more community-driven. Mayor of Lockhart River, Wayne Butcher, said, 'Our agenda is our communities, that's where we need to be; that's where we need to talk and that's where we need to make decisions. It's about community-driven agendas and practical outcomes'.[7]

---

[7] 'New Alliance in unity working for stronger Cape York Communities' *Waanta Newsletter* of Lockhart River Sept 2013, http://statements.qld.gov.au/Statement/Id/53104

Aboriginal and Torres Strait Islander Commission (ATSIC)

ATSIC, which was a national Indigenous elected body established by the federal government, was abolished in 2004 leaving no elected national Indigenous body. The administrative arm that supported it was also abolished so that there was and still is no dedicated federal department of Indigenous affairs. The move was to mainstreaming. The National Congress of Australia's First Nations was set up in 2010 but federal governments do not listen to it. It has been effective however in the United Nations arena.

Movement Back to Tribal Land

In the 1970s, there was a movement of Aboriginal groups back to their land from the artificially centralised communities or reserves that they had been forced onto by government or encouraged onto by missions. Living on another clan's land was sometimes a recipe for disputes. The federal Department of Aboriginal Affairs provided support to these homelands. The outstation or homelands movement was defined by a parliamentary committee as 'small decentralised communities of close kin established by the movement of Aboriginal people to land of social, cultural and economic significance to them ... The Committee has identified 588 homeland centre communities throughout Australia with a total population of about 9500'.[8] The outstation movement flourished at Aurukun.

In 1963, some Mapoon Aboriginal people were moved off their land north of Weipa by police when the government decided to close down the mission to make way for mining and they refused to move. One of those was Jean Jimmy who campaigned for them to return. I assisted them to do that in September 1974 with the help of Mick Miller, the Aboriginal Legal Service in Cairns and International

---

[8] *Return to Country, The Homelands Movement in Australia*, House of Representative Standing Committee on Aboriginal Affairs, March 1987

Development Action (IDA). It is still a thriving Aboriginal community today.[9]

When I returned from Mapoon, where I accompanied them on the move back, I was greeted at Mick Miller's home by a group of Aboriginal people from Yarrabah who wanted to move back to Buddabadoo and wanted to hear the story of how Mapoon did it. Encouraged, they moved back to Buddabadoo, about 30 km south of Yarrabah, a week later. Their telegram to Senator Cavanagh, the Minister for Aboriginal Affairs read:

> We wish to inform you of the return of Yedinji people to tribal land at Buddabadoo on Saturday, September 28, 1974. We urge you to take immediate action to stop Queensland DAIA from building a road through Yedinji tribal ground at Buddabadoo to Pine Creek for tourist purposes also tourist development at Kunggurra on Yedinji land must be stopped.

The telegram was signed by Fred Mundraby and Parmines Mundraby, tribal elders, and Mark Noble, Chairman, Yedinji Tribal Council.[10]

The Land Act (Aboriginal and Islander Land Grants) Amendment Act 1982

I cover in detail the introduction of the Land Act (Aboriginal and Islander Land Grants) Amendment Act 1982 which was passed in April that year and amended in 1984 and the response of Yarrabah to it and the infringements of human rights it entailed. The Deeds of Grant in Trust (DOGITs) it provided for were not, however, actioned till 1986 at Yarrabah. The council became the trustees for the land

---

[9] Roberts, J, Russell, B, Parsons, M (1975) eds. *The Mapoon Story by the Mapoon People.* Vol. 1 of 3 vols.

[10] "Yedinji Tribe Move Back to Buddabadoo" by Brian Gunn *The Cairns Post* 30/9/1974

which the community now owned communally. Despite Yarrabah's misgivings, it was a huge leap forward to having no land ownership at all.

After state elections in October 1983, the new Minister for Northern Development and Aboriginal and Islander Affairs, Bob Katter, made a speech in parliament where the word 'land rights' was used for the first time. I can almost hear the shudders of dismay that went through the government members. Katter introduced amendments to the Land Act and during the second reading, 'proposals embodied in this Bill will bring into the area of Aboriginal land rights a tenure adequate for the real long-term needs of people on the Aboriginal reserves in Queensland'. There was no love lost between Katter and Killoran, the hated and feared Director of the Department of Aboriginal and Islander Advancement (DAIA). From 1984–1989, it was known as the Department of Community Services (adding Ethnic Affairs in 1987). Further amendments to the Act occurred in 1986, 1987 and 1988. Later amendments to the Act meant that the government could only change the title deed by Act of Parliament.

Aboriginal Land Act 1991

When the Goss Labor government came into power in Queensland in December 1989, it moved quickly to fulfil its promises of Aboriginal land rights. I was working as the Secretariat Director or CEO of the Aboriginal Coordinating Council and wrote a quick response on behalf of the Queensland trust communities based on community input. The Aboriginal and Torres Strait Islander Commission (ATSIC), a national elected body representing urban and remote Aborigines established by the Commonwealth Government in 1990, made representations. However, ATSIC was given one month to make final submissions with no discussion paper. Marcia Langton and Noel Pearson were engaged by the state government to advise them on the Aboriginal Land Act. Noel had by this time formed the

Cape York Land Council to lobby for the interests of traditional owners on Cape York.

Some saw this body as competing with the Aboriginal Coordinating Council as the ACC represented the interests of Aboriginal local government councils who were the trustees of deeds of grant in trust. That is, they represented Aboriginal people who had historical as well as traditional ties to the ex-reserve land. Many Aboriginal people had a history of being forcibly removed from their traditional lands onto reserves and some inter-married with traditional owners. Some communities adopted a position that if you were born on a place, that was your home. The short consultation period caused Noel Pearson to resign.

The legislation was rushed through parliament which sat till 2 am, 30 May 1991, to pass it through all stages. A similar act, the Torres Strait Land Act 1991, was passed the next day. Frank Brennan had advised Catholic Bishops and Aboriginal groups on their submissions and he highlighted that the claims process didn't include urban areas. A land tribunal would be set up to hear land claims on reserves, DOGITs, Aurukun and Mornington Island or state land the government declared transferable. Claims could be on the basis of traditional or historical affiliation or on the basis of living on the land. Urban Aboriginal people missed out.

As of June 2016, 4.5 million hectares of land have been transferred and it is held in trust for the group of Aboriginals associated with that land and their descendants in inalienable freehold title. This means the land can't be sold or mortgaged and leasing of it is restricted. This has caused some issues with leasing of land for private homes or businesses. It does not extinguish native title. The state government retains mining and petroleum rights and some quarrying and forestry rights.

Mabo and Native Title 1992-1993

Eddie Koiko Mabo from Murray Island or Mer in the Torres Strait had been banished from Mer at age fifteen years for one year after clashing with Killoran. He moved to Townsville as an adult. In 1981, he spoke at a land rights conference in Townsville on the Torres Strait becoming an autonomous area within the Commonwealth and not being under state government control. Barbara Hocking, a Melbourne barrister, recommended Aboriginal people take up a test case for their tribal lands and Murray Island took up the case. They had already refused to accept a DOGIT from the Queensland Government as they didn't believe it was appropriate.

The test case began in 1982. Rev Dave Passi and James Rice from Mer joined Eddie Mabo in the case. Greg McIntyre was the solicitor for Mabo and his barristers were Ron Castan and Dr Bryan Keon-Cohen, with Barbara Hocking on the case for the first five years. The first hurdle was that Premier Joh Bjelke-Petersen tried to retrospectively extinguish native title rights in the Torres Strait. Mabo v Queensland (No 1) was decided in the High Court on 8 December 1988. It found that the Queensland Coast Islands Declaratory Act, which attempted to retrospectively abolish native title rights, was not valid according to the Racial Discrimination Act 1975.

After a long battle, in June 1992 the decision of the High Court in Mabo v Queensland (no 2) was that 'the Meriam people were entitled as against the whole of the world to the possession, occupation, use and enjoyment of (most of) the land of the Murray Islands in the Torres Strait'.[11] The High Court held that the common law of Australia recognises a form of native title to land so that this could be applied to the mainland as well. This was a ground-breaking decision as it overturned the notion of 'terra nullius' which was that Australia was a no man's land at the time of European settlement. This notion

---

[11] Miller, Barbara (1994) Options for the Future, Local Government and Native Title on Queensland Aboriginal Communities. Aboriginal Coordinating Council, P59.

had been confirmed in Millirrpum v Nabalco 1971 or the Gove Land Rights Case, the first of its kind in Australia, where Justice Blackburn found against the Aboriginal people. The Mabo decision meant that native title was held to exist where Aboriginal and Torres Strait Islander people have maintained their connection to their land and where government action has not extinguished their title. Eddie Mabo died a few months before this decision in his favour.

The Commonwealth Government enacted the Native Title Act in 1993 (Cth) and the Queensland Government followed suit with the Native Title Act 1993 (Qld) putting a legislative framework around the Mabo decision and instituting a mechanism for hearing claims. The Queensland legislation was enacted to amend other state legislation to bring it into alignment with the federal legislation. Prime Minister Paul Keating spoke of the wide-ranging importance of the Act on its second reading on 16 November 1993:

> For today, as a nation, we take a major step towards a new and better relationship between Aboriginal and non-Aboriginal Australians. We give the indigenous people of Australia, at last, the standing they are owed as the original occupants of this continent, the standing they are owed as seminal contributors to our national life and culture: as workers, soldiers, explorers, artists, sportsmen and women—as a defining element in the character of this nation—and the standing they are owed as victims of grave injustices as people have survived the loss of their land and the shattering of their culture.[12]

---

[12] Parliament of Australia, Native Title Bill 1993 Second Reading 16 November 1993 http://parlinfo.aph.gov.au/parlInfo/search/display/display.w3p;adv=yes;ord erBy=_fragment_number,doc_date-rev;query=Dataset%3Ahansardr,hansardr80%20Decade%3A%221990s%22%20Yea r%3A%221993%22%20Month%3A%2211%22%20Day%3A%2216%22%20Speaker_ Phrase%3A%22mr%20keating%22;rec=2;resCount=Default

Prescribed Body Corporates (PBCs) have been recognised regionally to be the bodies which deal with native title and Yarrabah has two PBCs. It is also a member of the North Queensland Land Council (NQLC, a later body that is government recognised and funded) not the one founded by Mick Miller, Clarrie Grogan, Peter Noble and myself in January 1977 before such legislative recognition and funding was possible in Queensland. The 1977 body represented an area now covered by Cape York Land Council and the North Queensland Council but only as far south as Palm Island and Townsville. The current NQLC, set up in 1994, is the Native Title Representative Body (NTRB) and its area extends from the Daintree and Bloomfield Rivers in the north to just SE of Sarina and west to beyond Richmond and Croydon and extends east to include waters that are within the Exclusive Economic Zone of Australia.

Yarrabah Was Nearly Mabo Two Test Cases

The Mabo court case and decision was a defining and watershed moment for the nation of Australia. It could so easily have been the Neal or Yarrabah case as well as Mabo. One of the barristers for the case, Bryan Keon-Cohen, revealed this in an article he wrote in 2000:

> Initially, work proceeded on developing two cases: one for Mer, another for the Yarrabah community, located on an aboriginal reserve in Far North Queensland. Meetings and preliminary advices in mid-September 1981 raised these prospects[13] and by March 1982, two draft statements of claim had been prepared[14]. However, for reasons uncertain to me, but apparently associated with a death in the community in June 1982,[15] and difficulties in obtaining instructions, the Yarrabah aboriginal action faded away. Alternatively, perhaps

---

[13] See Barbara Hocking, 'Preliminary Advice' (29 October 1981) *MC* vol. 5.
[14] Barbara Hocking, 'Memorandum' (11 March 1982) *MC* vol. 5.
[15] Bryan Keon-Cohen, 'Letter to Ron Castan' (7 June 1982) *MC* vol. 5.

the complexity—and the expense—of running two such cases
quickly became apparent, and all too much to contemplate.
Some hard decisions were doubtless taken, somewhere, by
somebody. Yet another explanation sometimes heard is that
instructions from Yarrabah were coming mainly from one Mr
Neal—who was 'entitled to be an agitator' *Neal v The
Queen* [1982] HCA 55; (1982) 149 CLR 305, 317 (Murphy J)—
but who, during this period, was notoriously jailed by a local
Magistrate for spitting through a wire-screen door at a police
officer.[16]

Percy Neal was chairman of Yarrabah Council and was elected on
a self-management platform but Yarrabah was still under the
infamous Queensland Act. His council's appeals to the
Commonwealth Government to take over control from the state using
its powers gained in the 1967 referendum fell on deaf ears. Frustrated,
he visited a number of homes of white staff one evening and asked
them to vacate the community. When he went to the home of store
manager Daniel Collins, it was alleged Neal used threatening and rude
language and spat at Collins through the screen door. He was
sentenced to two months' jail in the Cairns Magistrates Court. He
appealed and instead of having his sentence reduced, it was increased
to six months.

Chesterman and Villafor write:

This case became famous in September 1982 when the High
Court upheld Neal's appeal against the Court of Criminal
Appeal decision ... (Justice) Murphy then made the following
famous remarks: 'That Mr. Neal was an "agitator" or stirrer in
the magistrate's view obviously contributed to the severe

---

[16] BA Keon-Cohen, 'The Mabo Litigation: A Personal and Procedural Account'
[2000] MelbULawRw 35; (2000) 24(3) *Melbourne University Law Review* 893,
http://www.austlii.edu.au/au/journals/MelbULawRw/2000/35.html

penalty. If he is an agitator, he is in good company. Many of the great religious and political figures of history have been agitators, and human progress owes much to the efforts of these and the many who are unknown'.[17]

The same article maintains that Justice Murphy thought a $130 fine would have been a more appropriate sentence. However, Percy Neal served two months' jail. He was later to become a long-serving mayor of Yarrabah and lead it into self-management and local government. However, his court case and jail term did prevent Yarrabah being in the historic position that Mer was re native title and Percy Neal being in the historic position of Eddie Mabo or sharing that ground-breaking history with him.

I have spoken to Percy recently as I had been told that it was not Percy who spat through the screen door in frustration but his companion. Percy confirmed this and said that his companion was prevented in getting to the court case in time by two flat tyres and Percy has protected his name through concerns his friend could still be charged. Percy thinks he was marked by the state. He says, 'A policeman came to Yarrabah and said that if I agreed to resign and dissolve the council, then they would drop the case against me. I couldn't do that. Our self-determination was too important'.

Percy blames himself for the Community Development Employment Program (CDEP) being removed from Yarrabah in 2009 while he was mayor. Even though Yarrabah was not singled out as there were 2,000 CDEP places around Australia lost, 500 of these were at Yarrabah, a high proportion. Percy said he had criticised Indigenous Affairs Minister Jenny Macklin for promising funding for programs and not delivering and wondered whether Yarrabah had been targeted for this reason. He told me, 'I saw people devastated by this. It took them about five years to readjust. They were used to getting up early

---

[17] *Mr Neal's Invasion: Behind an Indigenous Rights Case,* John Chesterman and George Villaflor, http://www.austlii.edu.au/au/journals/AUJILawSoc/2000/1.pdf.

for work and having bills like electricity taken out of their pay. Jobs are hard to get and it meant a higher level of welfare dependency on our community' (August 2016 interview).

Current deputy mayor of Yarrabah, Michael Sands, says, 'Percy shouldn't blame himself. I was on council with him at the time and our remote status was removed even though in Yarrabah we had no bus, no taxi, no chemist etc.' (meeting with council 14/9/16). There were virtually no private enterprises on Yarrabah to employ people. Percy remembers council had about 300 CDEP workers and co-operative Bama Ngappi Ngappi had about 200.

Wik Claim

Before the Native Title Act was passed in December 1993, and with the help of the Cape York Land Council, the Wik and Thayorre people put in a native title claim in western Cape York that included two pastoral leases. The government believed that pastoral leases extinguished native title. The Federal Court found against the claim in January 1996 but an appeal to the High Court went in favour of the Wik claim in December 1996. It was found that pastoral leases did not extinguish native title but that pastoral rights had priority over native title rights so there were co-existing rights. There was great excitement from supporters with Gladys Tybingoompa from Aurukun dancing in front of Parliament House in Canberra. However, it caused a lot of controversy especially in Queensland and Western Australia.

The Commonwealth Government response to opposition to the Wik decision was to water it down with its Ten Point Plan. The Native Title Amendment Act 1998 was passed in July 1998 after heated debate. Claims were now to be lodged with the Federal Court with the National Native Title Tribunal assisting with mediation. There was a policy shift to negotiated agreements rather than litigation. One of the outcomes of this has been Indigenous Land Use Agreements (ILUAs) where native title claimants, their PBCs, government and industries affected would work out detailed agreements, usually a slow process.

The Western Cape Communities Co-Existence Agreement of 14 March 2001 is a ground-breaking example where eleven traditional owner groups, four Aboriginal councils, Cape York Land Council, mining company Comalco and the Queensland Government made an ILUA recognising native title interests, providing for return of land not used for mining, promises of consultation over future development and provision of funding for employment and training.

Indigenous Land Corporation (ILC)

The third major process for returning land to Indigenous people, after land rights legislation and native title, is land purchase, and, as a federal initiative, the Indigenous Land Corporation began buying land in 1995 to transfer to Indigenous owners. In 2010–11, it purchased five properties totalling about 337,000 hectares, including the Ayers Rock Resort at Uluru.

Aboriginal Land Fund Commission and the Koowarta Case

The Aboriginal Land Fund Commission predated the ILC being set up in 1974 by the Whitlam government to assist communities to acquire land outside reserves. John Koowarta and the Winychanam group approached the commission to buy their traditional land, part of the Archer River Pastoral Holding. The sale required the consent of the Queensland Government but they refused to give it, citing a Cabinet decision of 1972 that the government did not favour the acquisition of large areas of land by Aborigines 'in isolation' (Qld Parliament 1976, 2008).

Koowarta's legal team lodged a writ in the Supreme Court of Queensland claiming that the minister's decision contravened the Racial Discrimination Act of 1975 (RDA). The case of Koowarta v. Bjelke-Petersen, Tomkins, Glasson, and the State of

Queensland began in 1981 and the High Court in May 1982 decided that the RDA was valid and that Koowarta was an aggrieved person under the Act. Though Koowarta had won his case, he would never occupy his land because in 1977 the Queensland Government had gazetted it as a national park (later named Archer Bend National Park) and he passed away. In 2012, a later Queensland Government transferred it to Aboriginal ownership, partly as national park and partly as freehold.

It was a landmark case setting a precedent. Prime Minister Paul Keating commented that without John Koowarta 'there would have been no Mabo case, no native title legislation'.[18]

Private Economy and Home Ownership

It has not been possible for Aboriginal people living on Aboriginal communities in Queensland and other states to own land individually so that they can build a house on it which their children can inherit. Also, they've not been able to lease land to establish a business. It means that loans from traditional bank sources aren't possible and loans can only be made through the government's Indigenous Business Australia (IBA). It has also meant people living in social housing and a large reliance on CDEP jobs as there aren't enterprises to employ them. This is changing finally with ninety-nine year leases for private housing and business being introduced.

Yarrabah had its first case in 2014 where a resident was able to buy her own home. It has been leading the way with Indigenous businesses. I remember the Neal family being involved in a co-operative bakery in Yarrabah back in the 1970s followed later by a service station. Over the years, there has been a take-away food shop and today there is a coffee shop and newly established hairdresser.

---

[18] 'Aurukun Marks Land Win.' *The Courier-Mail*, 10 November 1993, 14). John Koowarta is the 'Mabo of the Mainland'.

Yarrabah is used to thinking big. On 18 June 2014, Yarrabah's Mayor Errol Neal and two councillors went to China on a ten-day trade mission in the hope of interesting potential investors in building a cruise-ship terminal, international airport and cultural precinct at Yarrabah. They were joined by representatives from Palm Island and Stradbroke Island. Yarrabah Council has erected a sign saying 'Paradise by the Sea' and it has beautiful scenery where the rainforest meets the beach.

Native Title for Gunggandji people of Yarrabah 2011

To clarify, in my consultations in Yarrabah in 1984, the Gunggandji people were spelling it Kongkandji and the Yidinji were spelling it Yedinji.

On 19 December 2011, the Gunggandji people of Yarrabah were recognised as the native title holders of more than 7500 hectares of land in Australia's 176th native title determination—sixty-six of which had been recognised in Queensland. The determination was the result of claims first lodged by the Gurubana Gunggandji and Les Murgha and Vincent Schrieber (Gunggandji People) in 1994 and 1995 respectively. Seven Indigenous Land Use Agreements (ILUAs) with the state and other interests outline how the rights of the various parties will be managed.

Principal lawyer Rachel Woolley said, 'The area covers about 7528 hectares of land and waters, including the northern part of the Yarrabah Deed of Grant in Trust; including the Yarrabah township, the foreshores of Mission Bay, Cape Grafton, Turtle Bay, Wide Bay and Oombunghi Beach, part of Malbon Thompson Forest Reserve and two parcels of land on Fitzroy Island'.[19]

A press release from the minister responsible, Mr Curtis Pitt, explained the native title decision's effect on DOGIT:

---

[19] http://www.crownlaw.qld.gov.au/resources/publications/queenslands-66th-native-title-win-for-indigenous-people

29

The Federal Court has formally recognised their exclusive native title rights over the northern part of the Yarrabah Deed of Grant in Trust (DOGIT) including Rocky Island. It also recognises non-exclusive native title rights over the northern part of the Yarrabah Deed of Grant in Trust (DOGIT) including reserves, unallocated State land, part of Trinity Forest Reserve and part of the Malbon Thompson Conservation Park.[20]

Joint MY-Gunggandji Native Title Determination 2012

The 74th Native Title determination in Queensland is the Combined Mandingalbay Yidinji-Gunggandji claim determined in Cairns on the 21 September 2012. The 82 km^2 of land includes the southern part of the Yarrabah DOGIT, some other areas of land around Yarrabah, and Gunjurra Island. The land is south of the Gunggandji claim which was finalised in 2011 and is east of the Malbon Thompson Range.

Exclusive rights to hunt, fish and hold ceremonies on the land following their traditional customs is recognised and three ILUAs were negotiated to manage cultural heritage and future ventures.[21]

Land Transfer Yarrabah 2015

In December 2015, State Treasurer Curtis Pitt announced that over 8000 hectares were added to Yarrabah's inalienable freehold title, in a move that would aid the economic viability of the community.

Chairman of the Gunggandji Mandingalbay Yidinji Peoples Aboriginal Corporation, Vince Mundraby, said:

---

[20] http://www.curtispitt.com.au/2011/12/19/combined-gunggandji-people%E2%80%99s-native-title-rights-recognised-at-yarrabah/
[21] *Djunbunji Land and Sea Program* News, http://www.djunbunji.com.au/news/yarrabah-title-determination/

Now ... it will be managed properly, the right way, the Gunggandji and Mandingalbay Yidinji Peoples way, our way. This will enable our community to develop an environmental economy, using our land, people and culture while transmitting to future generations a sustainable economy in a culturally appropriate manner that delivers a better quality of life.[22]

Transfer of Land on Foundation Day Celebrations 2016

In a striking coincidence, 7000 ha of land were transferred to the Gunggandji people 17 June 2016 on Foundation Celebrations. It was 124 years since Yarrabah was established as an Anglican mission by Reverend John Gribble. It was certainly a time for celebration as the entire headland of Yarrabah was returned to the town's traditional owners, ending a struggle for land rights going back to the 1970s and creating opportunities, both cultural and economic.

Frederick Noble, chairman of the Gunggandji Prescribed Body Corporate Aboriginal Corporation, welcomed the transfer, which came five years after a native title determination for the area. 'Receiving the deeds to our land means we're in control of our future and that of our younger generations.'[23]

Yarrabah Mayor Ross Andrews said:

There is a new paradigm shift of the management of the land from the council to the Gunggandji PBC and we must all be prepared to embrace these changes. Council and the Gunggandji PBC Aboriginal Corporation have committed to

---

[22] 'New Opportunities for Yarrabah after land transfer' Dominic Geiger, *The Cairns Post* 21/12/15 http://www.cairnspost.com.au/news/cairns/new-opportunities-for-yarrabah-after-land-transfer/news-story/
[23] '7000 ha land returned to Yarrabah traditional owners, the Gunggandji' by Kimberley Vlasic, *The Cairns Post* 18/6/16 http://www.cairnspost.com.au/news/cairns/7000ha-land-returned-to-yarrabah-traditional-owners-the-gunggandji/news-story/

work together to continue to create home ownership opportunities for residents.[24]

Township land will continue to be managed by Yarrabah Aboriginal Shire Council and home ownership lease arrangements will be available on transferred land and township land.

Native title negotiations have caused difficulty on a number of Aboriginal communities and Yarrabah is no exception. There are now three sets of trustees on Yarrabah with two native title bodies and the council. Through ILUAs, they have worked out how they can co-operate for a harmonious future.

Spiritual as well as Political Revival at Yarrabah

Yarrabah is a unique community in that it has a large number of Aboriginal Anglican priests and has Australia's first Aboriginal Anglican Bishop—Bishop Arthur Malcolm. Some of these priests have served on the elected Aboriginal local government council as well, notably Fr Wayne Connolly who was chairman of the council for a number of years and Fr Mick Connolly who was deputy chairman at the time of my 1984 study and has been chairman since. So the priests have been generally very active in community development, like Fr Les Baird who founded the community-controlled health centre there. Yarrabah has also known more than one spiritual revival with the children seeing visions.

Fr Les puts many of the positive changes in the community to God's intervention and recommended a look at Lynne Hume's work.[25] He says:

> After segregation virtually came to an end, God intervened and has done miraculous work in the community. It was the church group who founded the alcohol rehab centre and the

---

[24] ibid.
[25] Hume, Lynne (1989) *Yarrabah: Christian Phoenix, Christianity and Social Change on an Australian Aboriginal Reserve*. PhD Thesis.

health centre, both community controlled. From 1984 till now, God has given us back the land and community control of our own affairs. God has blessed our community.

When the government took control off the church, there were 14 outstations at Yarrabah and the government moved them back into the town area. Since our council has been running the community, people have moved back into those areas. We've been building out again. There are three main suburbs today—Djenghi, Murigan and Reeves Creek.[26]

In 1987, there were three deaths in custody at Yarrabah which helped spark the Royal Commission into Aboriginal Deaths in Custody. In 1995, there were five suicides in one year but there has been pro-active intervention in the community from church and council addressing this as well as programs to tackle domestic violence. Fr Les had led the push to introduce healing methods from North American Indian communities as well. Yarrabah has a women's group, men's group, youth group and women's centre but it is the strong spiritual focus of the community that has brought breakthrough.

'We have a lot of tertiary educated residents at Yarrabah and community control is operating in all aspects of the community except the school. We would like to have more say over the hospital but we do run the community health. Basically however, we have achieved all the things we dreamed about. It shows that given a chance to run our community, we can do it ourselves', said Fr Les.

---

[26] All comments from Les Baird here are part of a personal communication, August 2016.

SUMMARY

———◦———

T here has been much rhetoric about land rights and self-management/self-determination on both sides of the public debate. Rarely has there been a detailed examination of what these issues mean in concrete terms for an Aboriginal community. This examination of the aspirations of Yarrabah Aborigines in relation to local management and human rights inevitably produces such a document, for these are the central concerns of Queensland Aboriginal communities. Any such consultation with an Aboriginal community in Queensland at this point of time must focus on an analysis of the Community Services (Aborigines) Act 1984 (Q1d) and the Land Act (Aboriginal and Islander Land Grants) Amendment Act 1984 (Qld) to see to what extent these Acts satisfy or discount Aboriginal aspirations and increase or infringe their basic human rights.

Community Services (Aborigines) Act

Aboriginal aspirations at Yarrabah suffered a blow with the ramming through Queensland Parliament of the Community Services (Aborigines) Bill on 13 April 1984. The Yarrabah Council sent a telegram to the federal government four days later asking it to 'take over and fund Yarrabah reserve for the people of Yarrabah and implement self-management and the minister's five principles regarding land rights ...'

Three weeks later a reply was received that model land rights legislation would not be enacted before 1985 (after the next federal election) and that a meeting with Mr Katter, the Queensland minister, was being arranged to discuss Yarrabah.[27]

The council then decided to work with the Community Services (Aborigines) Act under protest because there seemed to be no alternative. Certain amendments were, however, requested.

At a small public meeting on 18 May 1984, residents sent a similar telegram to Canberra and a petition was circulated which over 400 people (over 60 per cent of the adults) signed.

The crux of the dissatisfaction with the Community Services (Aborigines) Act is that it does not give self-management. As the Chairman of Yarrabah, Roy Gray, says, 'It is only a name change, not a real change', with the Director of the Department of Aboriginal and Islander Advancement (DAIA) becoming the under-secretary of the Department of Community Services (DCS), and the (white) manager becoming the executive officer. The Yarrabah Council wanted the balance of power to change so that the council would run the community, not the executive officer, who would have the same role as a shire clerk. The council wanted departmental staff seconded to it for up to three years to facilitate the changeover. However the Community Services (Aborigines) Act has maintained a situation where there are two administrations—the department and its staff with most of the power, and the council and its staff. The executive officer has to approve each and every expenditure of Queensland Government grants.[28]

The other matter of great dissatisfaction to the Yarrabah community is the Aboriginal Industries Board (AIB), on which there was no consultation by government beforehand. Previously, income from enterprises on communities did not go back into the community

---

[27] Telegram to Cr Roy Gray, Chairman of Yarrabah Council from Mr Clyde Holding, Federal Minister for Aboriginal Affairs on 9 May 1984. Unpublished held by Yarrabah Council.
[28] Yarrabah Council Meeting, Yarrabah 9 April 1984. Author's unpublished record. See Community Services (Aborigines) Act (Qld) s.24 (b).

fund but into the Aborigines Welfare Fund controlled by the government to service all the communities. That body continues to exist but this function, which is deeply resented, will be taken over by the AIB. From an Aboriginal point of view the situation is not helped by the fact that Mr Pat Killoran, the under-secretary, is the chairman, and the Governor-in-Council will appoint three (probably non-Aborigines) to the board of nine; the other five being appointed by the Aboriginal Co-ordinating Council which consists of the chairmen of all reserves/trust areas, and replaces the Aboriginal Advisory Council. The latter body voted at its Weipa meeting in May to have Mr Killoran removed from the department.[29] There is no guarantee that a Yarrabah person will be on the AIB. The minister may recommend to the Governor-in-Council that an administrator replace AIB members without specifying a reason. The administrator can run the AIB for up to two years.

The Yarrabah Council had requested that all assets of DAIA/DCS be handed over to it and that the council decide which enterprises would be run in the Yarrabah community by it, private individuals or the co-operative. However DCS is retaining some enterprises, and handing some over to the AIB which can gradually divest them to councils and individuals.

The dual management of Yarrabah by the DAIA/DCS and the Aboriginal council is causing great distress on Yarrabah because their priorities are different; DCS has most of the power and the executive officer on Yarrabah is not interested in divesting management power to Aborigines but is *frustrating* the council's steps at every point. The chairman of Yarrabah, Councillor Roy Gray, said:

> There could be two separate developments at Yarrabah—two water pipes, two roads, two lots of machinery.

---

[29] Statement made to author in discussion with Yarrabah Council, May 1984. Author's unpublished record.

We thought we needed the DCS to help phase self-management in but it is not working out that way. The Department seems to be in competition with us.[30]

There are many other complaints by Yarrabah Aborigines against the Community Services (Aborigines) Act which they feel infringes basic human rights:

1. Significant departures from the Local Government Act in the area of financial accountability, which constitute *inequality before the law.*

2. *Self-determination* which is a basic human right is denied, e.g. the minister can dissolve an elected council in his absolute discretion; and there is no time limit before fresh elections.

3. The old by-laws are still in force for the time being and they infringe the right of *freedom of assembly.*

4. Although the Community Services (Aborigines) Act makes no mention of *award wages*, these are still not being paid to DCS workers. Sacked DAIA workers are having difficulties at the moment with *long service leave entitlements.*

5. Residents cannot elect to go to a magistrates court for by-law and regulations infringements. They must go before an Aboriginal court. Public servants automatically go before a magistrates court. This constitutes *inequality before the law.*

---

[30] Statement by Cr Roy Gray, Chairman of Yarrabah Council to the author at informal meeting between author and some Yarrabah Councillors, Council office, Yarrabah, July 1984. The purpose of the meeting was the approval by Yarrabah Council of this report for publication. It was requested this comment be added. Author's unpublished record.

6. *The right to inherit* is infringed by the Community Services (Aborigines) Act which provides that if an Aborigine dies without appointing an executor, or an Aborigine is missing, the under-secretary decides who succeeds to his or her estate or whether anybody does.

7. *The right to housing* is a basic human right. There is a great housing need at Yarrabah. Although self-management has been met by giving the council responsibility for housing, the threat is that the resources will not be there from Queensland Government public housing funds to make this meaningful.

8. The Yarrabah community has been discriminated against in the unequal provision of *educational facilities* by the Queensland Government which has refused to provide covered walkways and a covered lunch area for the high school students to protect them from heavy summer rains and heat.

9. To achieve equality before the law, consonant with the principles of self-determination, the Liquor Act should apply on Yarrabah.

10. The Community Services (Aborigines) Act allows the council and courts to take Aboriginal culture into account, but tribal and customary marriages are no longer recognised by the Queensland Government. Special provisions for recognising *tribal and customary law* principles in the administration of the estates of intestate Aboriginals have also been left out.

11. The provision for visiting justices to report on communities to the under-secretary every three months on any matter on which he requests a report, and the ability of the under-secretary to appoint 'any person' to hold inquiries smacks of an Orwellian (Big Brother) type

scrutiny of communities like Yarrabah and constitutes *racial discrimination*.

There is concern among some Yarrabah residents that under s.18 of the Community Services (Aborigines) Act, they will be struck off the roll and ineligible to vote for or stand for Mulgrave Shire Council elections if they are on the voters' roll for Yarrabah Council elections. This is despite the fact that the Community Services (Aborigines) Act is only a parody of local government and in some ways gives fewer rights to Aborigines than they had before. However, the Yarrabah Council approves s.18 because they cannot see any advantage to Yarrabah residents in voting for the Mulgrave Shire Council and they do not want any interference by Mulgrave Shire Council in Yarrabah. Yarrabah Council wants to operate as autonomously as possible. To some extent, there is a tension here between human rights and self-determination.

The Community Services (Aborigines) Act is an improvement over previous legislation which required permits for visits to and residency in Yarrabah, thus infringing the right to freedom of movement of Aborigines out of favour with councils or, before 1975 (overriding Federal law), the DAIA.

There is a conflict of interests here between human rights and self-management because the Yarrabah Council would like to retain the permit system to ensure privacy and protect the land from incursion. The council can make by-laws to exclude a class of persons but the by-laws will have to accord with the Community Services (Aborigines) Act. Another human rights concern is that there is no right of appeal for persons excluded from the community.

Land Rights

The chairman of Yarrabah, Mr Roy Gray, aptly described the relationship between self-management and land rights when he asked, 'If we haven't got land rights, what've we got to manage anyway?'[31]

Under the Land Act (Aboriginal and Islander Land Grants) Amendment Act 1984 (Qld) (commonly referred to as the Deed of Grant in Trust legislation (DOGIT)), the Yarrabah community would be given the land presently reserved for it under a deed of grant in trust with the council as trustees.

The Yarrabah Council wrote to the Minister for Aboriginal and Island Affairs, Mr Bob Katter, on 26 January 1984 and requested the following amendments to DOGIT (abbreviated here):[32]

1. The Council, not the Minister, should approve leases.

2. There should be no exclusions from the grant for departmental purposes. The Council should own all the land and grant occupancy to the Department.

3. Reservations from the grants for public purposes should not occur. If public works are to benefit Yarrabah, the Trustees would agree. Otherwise compulsory acquisition with compensation should apply.

4. The Government ought not to have the power to remove Trustees.

5. The Council wants the right to participate in and control mining, fishing, forestry, quarrying and the conduct of enterprises in general, and sea rights to a three-mile limit.

---

[31] Statement by Cr Roy Gray, Chairman of Yarrabah Council to the author at Yarrabah April 1984. Author's unpublished record.

[32] Letter to Minister for Aboriginal and Island Affairs, Mr Bob Katter from Cr Roy Gray, Chairman of Yarrabah Council on 26 January 1984. Unpublished, held by Yarrabah Council.

In other words, the Yarrabah Council does not want a piece of land with holes in it. In fact, there could be a lot more gaps in it if the government amends DOGIT to exclude commercial activity from the deed, i.e. give separate deeds to Aborigines as individuals or co-operatives for businesses or farms instead of their leasing land from the council as DOGIT now provides. Mr Katter has also foreshadowed giving Aborigines separate deeds to the land on which their houses are instead of their leasing from the council.[33]

The amount of community land will be severely eroded and so too will the ability of the council to make by-laws over the trust area. I believe this is a step towards the Queensland Government's plan of assimilation: the whittling away of Aboriginal community-owned land, so that in ten years or so, Yarrabah will be like another Queensland country town with a few extra black faces.

At the Yarrabah public meeting on 8 April 1984, those living outside the village at places like Back Beach and Buddabadoo expressed their worries about losing their land and being moved back into the village.[34] The share farmers are also scared that their land will be taken from them, despite assurances from the council. Some of the Kongkandji tribe are concerned that King Beach, an area of special significance, will be declared a public place and that a public road will be built to it. It was also felt that having staff housing excised from the trust area constituted segregation.

Basic principles recognised by federal governments, both Labor and Liberal, have not been addressed in this legislation except for the principle of inalienable freehold. Even then, it is not a deed of grant in fee simple or freehold. It is a deed of grant in trust which can be alienated by Act of Parliament to the Crown or transferred to another

---

[33] Queensland, Legislative Assembly, *Hansard* 1984, vol.294 12 April 1984. (The Minister's Second Reading Speech on the Community Services (Aborigines) Bill).
[34] Yarrabah Public Meeting on 8 April 1984. Author's unpublished record.

local authority if the trust is not complied with. It can also be alienated by mortgage default.

The Land Act (Aboriginal and Islander Land Grants) Amendment Act 1984, which is relevant only to large Aboriginal reserves that have a departmental presence—like Yarrabah—does not cover sacred sites, country reserves, Crown land, traditional land no longer reserved, or compensation. This leaves country reserves, which include over two-thirds of the Queensland Aboriginal population, in limbo.

Sacred sites are, however, dealt with in the Aboriginal Relics Preservation Act, but the sites covered by this Act are only those which have been modified by human intervention (e.g. rock art and archaeological sites). The Act also makes the sites the property of the Crown.

All mention of mining was omitted from the Community Services (Aborigines) Act and no provision made, as in the Aborigines Act, for negotiation of terms (e.g. a percentage of profits, as applies in the case of the Cape Flattery Silica Mine on the Hope Vale reserve). Under DOGIT, the government is only required to take into regard the views of the trustee but is not bound by them. Deeds of grant in trust occupiers have fewer rights than occupiers of Crown and private land who are entitled to compensation. Yarrabah Council is making moves to take out an authority to prospect but will have to get the permission of the Governor-in-Council. Mineral rights are enjoyed by some Queenslanders, but not by Aborigines.

Yarrabah Aborigines have fewer rights than holders of pastoral tenures in Queensland who have full quarry rights and forestry rights after two years. Yarrabah Aborigines have to apply and pay for a permit to collect firewood etc. The Community Services (Aborigines) Act protects hunting and fishing by traditional means for the people's own consumption, but gives no commercial rights. This means the Yarrabah Aborigines cannot keep commercial fishermen out of their waters.

There was little consultation with the Yarrabah Council over DOGIT. They have requested maps of the deed of grant areas to be prepared by the government in consultation with Council elders to prevent their being presented with a *fait accompli*. Yarrabah Council has formally claimed False Cape, Rocky Island, Green Island, Fitzroy Island and Little Fitzroy Island.

A great deal of bureaucratic control and political interference are built into both DOGIT and the Community Services (Aborigines) Act making full rights to land impossible: the Cabinet may remove one or all of the trustees if they consider it in the public interest; the trustees need the approval of the minister to grant leases; the minister determines rent; and by-laws of the trustees are subject to the veto of the minister. Leases are for seventy-five years, but the minister may cancel a lease and any improvements by a tenant become the property of the trustees, i.e. the Aboriginal council.[35]

Queensland Aboriginal laws have been, and still are, instruments of oppression and discrimination. Depending on the phase of Queensland Government policy, Queensland laws have also been instruments of segregation and assimilation. Equality means the right to be different and the right to equal opportunity for Aborigines to determine their own varied futures.

A landmark address was given by the deputy chairman of the Human Rights Commission, Mr Peter Bailey, to the Queensland Branch of the Institute of International Affairs in November 1983.

> There could be no more important advance in the area of race discrimination than for the Queensland Government to give Aboriginal people full rights to land and control over the lives of those living on that land ... Although much conscientious effort is devoted in Queensland to assist the Aboriginal people, structural changes are required, and much greater

---

[35] Land Act 1902–1978 (Qld), s.344 and s.348.

attentiveness to and active implementation of the wishes of the people themselves.

As this paper shows, there is a long way to go yet in Queensland before Aborigines on reserves/trust areas like Yarrabah have basic human rights. Although structural changes have occurred—DOGIT and the Community Services (Aborigines) Act—full rights to land and self-determination have not been achieved. Aboriginal aspirations have been largely ignored. Aborigines in Queensland have less rights at law than other Queenslanders and are subject to an Orwellian-type scrutiny that the rest of the community would not tolerate.

The federal government has a mandate to ensure that the human rights of Aborigines take precedence over state rights in Queensland as the Federal Minister for Aboriginal Affairs Mr Clyde Holding has assured us they would.

I.
INTRODUCTION

———————◊———————

The timing of this project was auspicious. Undertaken during mid-March to May 1984, it presented an opportunity to assess the aspirations of Yarrabah Aborigines both before and after the passage of Queensland Government legislation (13 April) purporting to give local management and the same rights enjoyed by other Queenslanders to Aborigines on Queensland reserves.

Aboriginal aspirations in Yarrabah can be crystallised in terms of two basic demands—land rights and self-determination. More politically aware Aborigines prefer to use the term self-determination rather than self-management. Self-determination means the power to make policy decisions over their lives while self-management simply means the right to make administrative decisions about policy which has been made over their heads. Most Aborigines use the terms synonymously. For Yarrabah, it means community control through a local elected Aboriginal council, not control by the under-secretary of the Department of Community Services through his local agent, a European executive officer (before May 31, the director of the Department of Aboriginal and Islander Advancement, and his local white manager).

The responses of Yarrabah Aborigines to the frustrations of their aspirations have varied from militancy, reformist action, co-operation with the system, to alcoholism. For some Aborigines, aspirations mean agitating for their goals, for others, pining over frustrated needs. Both these responses are unacceptable to the dominant white Australian culture. However, *these responses* to the frustration of Aboriginal aspirations will not be explored in this paper as they are beyond its scope.

Yarrabah is situated about 1727 km north-west of Brisbane, the capital of Queensland, and about 60 km by road from Cairns. The city of Cairns overlooks Trinity Bay and around the point, the Yarrabah village borders on Mission Bay. The Murray Prior Range separates the two communities which are much closer by boat than road. The dilapidated houses are in stark contrast to the beauty of the natural environment—sandy beaches with coconut trees and rugged rainforest-clad ranges.

About 1522 Aborigines live at Yarrabah. Originally set up in 1892 as a Church of England mission, it was handed over to Queensland Government administration in 1960. The reserve area has been whittled down to its present 154.4 km². (See Appendix A.)

An Aboriginal, according to the Racial Discrimination Act 1975 (Cwth), s.3 (1), means a person who is a descendant of an indigenous inhabitant of Australia but does not include a Torres Strait Islander.

A distinct cultural group, Torres Strait Islanders are often lumped together with Aborigines for legislative and administrative purposes because they are black and share the experience of colonisation with Aborigines. Although some of this paper could be applied to them, they do not come within the scope of this report.

Human rights for the purposes of this paper are defined as those set out in the Racial Discrimination Act and the international instruments relating to human rights and freedoms—the *International Convention on the Elimination of All Forms of Racial Discrimination* and the *International Covenant on Civil and Political Rights*.

This case study of Yarrabah will illuminate the issues of concern to Aborigines on all Queensland reserves at the present moment. It cannot be said that Yarrabah is typical, however, because its residents are generally more articulate and politicised than their counterparts in the more isolated northern reserves. Yarrabah, like Palm Island, is near a large urban centre and has more contact with the outside world.

II.
RESEARCH METHOD

A qualitative approach was chosen over a quantitative methodology because it is less directive, i.e. less likely to put words in people's mouths, than a questionnaire where people are forced to make a response. I did not have to create a research situation. I merely observed history in the making and reported it, looking at the implications for the future.

Time constraints meant that most of my consultation with the people of Yarrabah was through the Yarrabah Council, the elected Aboriginal body responsible for the community. I made nine (9) field trips to Yarrabah. The first was to obtain permission from the Yarrabah Council to visit the reserve for the duration of the project. I acquainted the Yarrabah Co-operative and some of the Buddabadoo group with the project and visited the manager and the hospital matron.

My second visit was to influential community members who did not know what was happening regarding the Community Services (Aboriginal) Act and they decided formally to request the council for a public meeting. This was held on 8 April with the Minister for Aboriginal and Island Affairs attending. That constituted my fifth visit. My third, sixth and eighth visits were to attend regular council meetings. At one of these, on 17 April, the council decided to send a telegram to the federal government asking them to take over the reserve. Mr Katter arrived on 19 April and held a confidential meeting to hear the council's complaints. I attended with officers of the Aboriginal Development Commission (ADC), Cairns, at the council's request. My fourth visit was to sit in on a meeting of the Yarrabah Council and the ADC to discuss Yarrabah's enterprise development plan. On 18 May 1984, I attended a public meeting at Yarrabah—my last visit for the project.

Two Yarrabah councillors came to workshops I organised in Cairns on 29–30 March and 6 April. The North Queensland Land Council called a Land Needs Conference in Cairns in March at which two Yarrabah councillors contributed.

Extensive background reading was necessary for this project because of the range of legislation which applied to Aborigines on Queensland reserves/trust areas. Yarrabah Council documents, parliamentary records, Aboriginal Advisory Council and DAIA records, where obtainable (a shroud of secrecy covers this type of information), and Frank Brennan's consultation documents were all useful as was some general historical and anthropological background reading (see Bibliography). Yarrabah's solicitor, Mr Greg McIntyre, provided valuable advice.

III.
HISTORICAL CONTEXT

The situation of Aborigines in North Queensland today (indeed, in Australia as a whole) can only be understood in terms of the Industrial Revolution and subsequent expansion of British colonial power. The search for resources and the need for a dumping ground for convicts—the victims of British industrialisation and urbanisation—led to the colonisation of what is now known as Australia.

Undeclared War

White settlement in Australia meant violent dispossession for Aborigines who had been here for tens of thousands of years. Settlers moved north from Sydney into what is now Queensland in about 1830. The government allowed settlers and native police to take the law into their own hands.

Non-Aboriginal claims to land frequently overrode the Aborigines' right to life.[36] Aborigines were seen as a doomed race, destined to disappear in the face of the superior white civilisation.[37] Outright slaughter, poisoning of flour and waterholes, introduction of disease and the banishment of Aborigines from traditional sources of food and water were the means of 'dispersal' used by the settlers.

---

[36] Prof. C.D. Rowley, The destruction of Aboriginal society, vol. 1, *Aboriginal policy and practice*, ANU Press, Canberra, 1970, p.154.
[37] Dr Noel Loos, *Aboriginal-European relations in North Queensland 1861–1897*. Ph.D. Thesis, James Cook University, Townsville, 1976, p.456.

Isolation and Protection

In the late 1890s, the use of Aborigines as a cheap labour pool gained force. They were employed as station hands or crewmen for fishing and pearling boats. However, the kidnapping of Aborigines to work on ships and their abandonment miles from home, child labour, disease, drunkenness and drug addiction led to the Queensland Government rounding up and 'relocating' Aborigines on reserves for their protection. Here (under the Aboriginals Protection and Restriction of the Sale of Opium Act 1897), they became wards of the State and had to have work permits to work outside the reserves and their property was managed by the State.

The purpose of this legislation was also to secure the development of Aborigines in isolation from the rest of the community. Miscegenation was curtailed by outlawing sex for unmarried Aborigines and requiring Aboriginal women to get the permission of the Chief Protector to marry.

This Act was revoked in 1939 and replaced by the Aboriginals Preservation and Protection Act, the Chief Protector becoming the Director, Native Affairs.

Assimilation Era

In the 1950s the policy of segregation lost currency and the Queensland Government decided to incorporate Aborigines as individuals into the mainstream of Australian society. It did not want to integrate Aborigines as groups nor did it envisage their maintaining distinct communities within the state.[38]

The Department of Aboriginal and Island Affairs (DAIA) was established by the Aboriginal and Torres Strait Islanders' Affairs Act of 1965 and it was to work itself out of a job. Reserves were to be

---

[38] Queensland Parliament, *Department of Native Affairs annual report 1963*, Parl. Paper 1061, Brisbane, 1963–64.

temporary training camps which would serve as springboards for Aboriginal incorporation into the wider community.

The plan was to eventually abolish the reserves and grant whichever communities might remain on them the legal status of Townships.[39] (A plural society was not to be created however. The Queensland Government saw Aboriginal culture as a handicap to the assimilation process. In 1978, the word 'assimilation' was dropped in favour of 'integration' but the substance of Queensland Government policy was unchanged.)

Pressure from Aborigines, the federal government and overseas was unable to secure more than minimal changes to the Queensland Aborigines Act 1971, which was amended in 1974, 1975 and 1979.

FAIRA Survey

In 1977, the Foundation for Aboriginal and Islanders Research Action (FAIRA) and the Aboriginals and Torres Strait Islanders Legal Service, Queensland, conducted a survey of Queensland Aborigines and 73.1 per cent of Aborigines on reserves wanted the Commonwealth Government to be responsible for making laws about Aboriginal reserves in Queensland. Only 14.5 per cent wanted the Queensland Government to continue its responsibility.[40]

Despite this, the Queensland Government extended the term of the Aborigines Act till 31 May 1984 on the basis of advice from its appointed Aboriginal and Islanders Commission. Mrs Rose Colless, its urban Aboriginal representative who submitted a minority dissenting submission, was sacked.

---

[39] Queensland, Parliament, *Department of Aboriginal and Island Affairs annual report 1968*, Parl. Paper 1102, Brisbane, 1968.

[40] Les Malezer, Matt Foley & Paul Richards, *Beyond the Act. Queensland Aborigines and Islanders: what do we want?* Foundation for Aboriginal and Islander Research Action Ltd, 1979, p.87.

Land and Services Legislation

A major focus of this report is to consider the aspirations of Aboriginal people on Yarrabah reserve regarding the new Services Legislation—the Community Services (Aborigines) Act 1984—and their reaction to what they received.

This legislation is complementary to the Land Act (Aboriginal and Islander Land Grants) Amendment Bill 1982 which is commonly referred to as the Deed of Grant in Trust legislation, and was enacted in early May 1984. Another major focus of this report is to assess Yarrabah Aboriginal aspirations regarding this land legislation.

The relationship of land rights to self-management was succinctly expressed by the chairman of Yarrabah, Mr Roy Gray: 'If we haven't got land rights, what have we got to manage anyway?'[41]

---

[41] Cr Roy Gray, Chairman of Yarrabah in a statement to author at Yarrabah April 1984. Author's unpublished record.

IV.
YARRABAH AND
SELF-MANAGEMENT

A. Queensland Aborigines Act

Under the Queensland Aborigines Act 1971–1979, which was operative till 31 May 1984, the reserves were run by a (white) manager under the Department of Aboriginal and Island Affairs (DAIA). People were not allowed to be on reserves (which are Crown land) unless they had a permit to visit or a permit to reside or were discharging functions under the Act. Copies of these permits appear at Appendix B. Permits could be granted by Aboriginal councils or the director where there was no council. The director or the council could revoke permits. Under the Aboriginal and Torres Strait Islanders (Queensland Discriminatory Laws) Act 1975 which is federal overriding legislation, Aborigines cannot be removed from reserves unless an Aboriginal council considers their conduct unreasonable.

The director of the DAIA could enter into mining agreements without consultation with Aboriginal residents of reserves and could negotiate terms for a share in the profits for the general benefit of Aborigines. The property of Aborigines could be managed if desired and harsh contracts made by businessmen with Aborigines could be cancelled by the director. Despite normal Queensland law, s.40 (a) of this State Act said that the director 'shall administer the estate of a deceased or missing Aborigine whose property was, at the time of his death or disappearance, being managed under s.37 of this Act and, if the nature or value of the estate requires a grant of probate or of letters of administration to be made, shall be entitled to that grant in priority to all other persons'.

Aboriginal police were appointed by the manager in consultation with the council and worked under the manager's direction. They could make arrests only for breaches of the regulations or the council by-laws.

B. Regulations

The regulations accompanying the Act made the council of five responsible to the manager and council by-laws had to be approved by the minister.[42] A person ceased to be a councillor if he/she was convicted in the Aboriginal court for any offence (s.34(d)) or if the minister thought he/she was physically or mentally sick (s.34(g)). An Aboriginal court consisting of two justices of the peace or three councillors dealt with breaches of the regulations or by-laws.

The Aborigines Welfare Fund was managed and controlled by the director and proceeds of the sale of produce resulting from commercial effort of communities and reserves (s.4(1)(c)) were paid into it (rather than income produced on a reserve staying on that reserve by being vested in a community fund). Such community funds were managed by councils but the director was trustee (s.42 (2)).

Regulation 84 controlled the supply of beer, other alcohol not being allowed on reserves. Councils were not authorised to have beer canteens open for more than four hours a day and were not allowed to sell take-home supplies. Aborigines living on a reserve were not permitted to be in the possession of beer or other liquor or to bring it onto the reserve.

---

[42] The Aborigines Regulations of 1972 (Qld), ss.18(1), 19.

C. By-Laws

These are supposedly the by-laws of Aboriginal councils but they are a standard set of by-laws produced by the DAIA and adopted by Aboriginal councils.[43]

D. Yarrabah Proposal Community Services (Aborigines) Legislation

At a meeting of the Yarrabah Council on 19 March 1984, the council's proposals of 9 June 1983 for inclusion in the new Community Services (Aborigines) Act were reviewed and the council submitted the following proposal to the Queensland Government:[44]

Council unanimously agreed on the following:

1. <u>COUNCIL</u>

(a) <u>Size of Council</u>
Council should comprise 7 members and a quorum should be 4 members.

(b) <u>Term of Office</u>
Should be 3 years. Non-Aborigines should not be eligible to vote.

(c) <u>Elections</u>

---

[43] Prof. Garth Nettheim, *Victims of the law: black Queenslanders today*, Allen & Unwin, Sydney, 1981, p.113, cited in Australia, Human Rights Commission, *Aboriginal reserves by-laws and human rights* (Occasional paper no. 5) AGPS, Canberra, 1983 p.22.

For a full discussion of the by-laws see Australia Human Rights Commission, *Aboriginal reserves by-laws and human rights* (Occasional paper no.5). Page 22 concludes, 'In their offensively intrusive nature, as well as their selected applicability to residents on reserves the by-laws are a clear form of discrimination'.
See Appendix D, Table 1: Human Rights Issues Raised by the Queensland By-Laws, p 131.
[44] Yarrabah Council Meeting Yarrabah, 19 March 1984. Attachment to Minutes. Unpublished, held by Yarrabah Council.

Eligibility to vote should be governed by either of the following criteria: being an Aboriginal person born at Yarrabah and resident there for 5 years out of the last 10 years; or being an Aboriginal person resident at Yarrabah for 1 year or more.

Chairman should be the person receiving the highest number of votes; Deputy Chairman should be the person receiving the second highest number of votes.

(d) Conditions
No amendment.

(e) Powers/Responsibilities
Council will require public servants posted to Yarrabah to be granted permits to live at Yarrabah; Council will grant such permits in first instance for 3 months only; at the expiry of 3 months, any public servant considered to be an undesirable resident will be issued a Notice to Show Cause why his or her Permit to Reside at Yarrabah should not be revoked, as per s.26 of the Aborigines Act 1971-79.

2. PERMITS
Council should retain powers of granting permits of residency— Council can delegate powers of issuing temporary permits to staff where necessary.

3. MANAGER AND COUNCIL
Council should have the full powers of a normal Town Council with the person employed as Executive Officer of the Council adopting the same role as that of a Shire Clerk.
Council acknowledges the need to retain the expertise at present provided by DAIA at Yarrabah.

Council will require selected DAIA personnel to be retained at Yarrabah on a secondment basis for up to 3 years but will also negotiate terms of secondment for individual public servants where the need arises.

4. COMMUNITY COURTS

Council wishes that there be constituted at Yarrabah a Magistrates Court comprising 2 or more Aboriginal Justices of the Peace and further that all moneys collected as a result of imposition of Court Fines be remitted to the Yarrabah Community Fund and that these moneys not be paid into Consolidated Revenue.

5. POLICE

Council considers Aboriginal Police should be retained at Yarrabah but that their training should be up-graded to State Police standards within a specially devised program for Aborigines.

6. CANTEEN AND ALCOHOL

Council wishes to be given the power to decide hours of operation of beer canteen and whether or not canteen should sell any type of liquor other than beer. Council should also become canteen licensee.

7. ADVISORY COUNCILS

Council wishes Advisory Councils to be retained and that DAA be requested to fund a small Secretariat. Council also wishes Councils to have the power to appoint sub-committees to investigate special issues.

8. ABORIGINAL AND ISLANDER COMMISSION

Council considers that non-reserve Aboriginal people should be provided for under separate legislation.

9. MISCELLANEOUS

Council recommends that Advisory Council representatives should be members of Archaeology Branch Board, to be set up under new legislation.

Council wishes Yarrabah people to continue to have the rights to hunt, fish etc. on the reserve unless the use of particular areas was otherwise set aside.

10. ADDITIONAL

(a) Disqualification of Councillors
Council considers that a Yarrabah resident should not be disqualified from nominating to stand as a Councillor unless he has been convicted of an indictable offence and that the wording 'serious offence' is too vague.

(b) Management of Property
Council resolved that the special provisions of the existing State Act regarding management of the property of Aboriginal people be abolished and that in future, management of property should be handled by the Yarrabah Magistrates Court.

(c) Grant-of-Aid
Council wishes that powers under s.36 of existing Act be transferred to Council.

(d) Welfare Fund

Council considers that any takeover of the Welfare Fund means an automatic takeover of all fixed assets, e.g. sawmill, store etc., plus any moneys still held after Fund has been audited and the books closed off.

(e) Other Assets

Council requests that on implementation of the new Act, all other buildings and items of plant presently owned by DAIA at Yarrabah be handed over to it.

(f) Withdrawal of services

Manager, DAIA, Yarrabah, considered Council should request the Minister to give an assurance to Council that no services be withdrawn from Yarrabah, on implementation of the new Community 'Services' (Aborigines) Act, without full consultation with Council. Council agrees with this and so requests the Minister.

E. Cairns Workshop 29–30 March 1984

The chairman and deputy chairman of Yarrabah attended a workshop at Kuiyam Hostel in Cairns organised for Cairns Aboriginal input into this project on 29–30 March 1984. The following resolution was moved by Joe McGuinness and seconded by the chairman of Yarrabah, Roy Gray:

That the Human Rights Commission request that a draft copy of the new Services Legislation be circulated widely by the Queensland Government for discussion amongst the Queensland community and that adequate consultation time be given to Aborigines on Queensland reserves.

This was passed unanimously by close to fifty Aborigines. (The full text of the resolutions passed at the workshops appears at Appendix C.)

F. Public Meeting Yarrabah 8 April 1984

A number of Yarrabah residents, including Mr Percy Neal of the Yarrabah Co-operative, signed a letter to the council requesting a public meeting because they wanted to know what was likely to be in the Community Services (Aborigines) Act and so that the public could have some input into it.[45] The council agreed somewhat reluctantly because it did not know what was going to be in the Community Services (Aborigines) Act either, although its hopes of achieving self-management were high. The council invited the Minister for Aboriginal and Island Affairs and Northern Development Mr Bob Katter.

Some highlights are included here to demonstrate the self-management concerns of Yarrabah Aborigines.[46]

Mr Lloyd Fourmile and Mr Colin Neal asked Mr Katter to tell the people what was in the Community Services (Aborigines) Act. But Mr Katter said that the legislation was secret until it went to the House. He was there not to tell the people but to listen to what they wanted.

The deputy chairman of Yarrabah, Cr Mick Connolly, said, 'The councillors are not stupid and I want to tell Mr Katter that the shroud of secrecy surrounding the legislation is not on. The people want to see a draft copy.' Mr Percy Neal also asked for a draft copy of the legislation.

Mrs Anna Palmer asked who would be in charge—the DAIA or the council, black or white. Cr Mick Connolly replied that the council wanted the manager to be hired and fired by it, not the DAIA, so that

---

[45] Letter to Yarrabah Council from residents of Yarrabah, April 1984. Unpublished, held by Yarrabah Council.

[46] Yarrabah Council Public Meeting, Yarrabah, 8 April 1984. Minutes. Author's record, unpublished.

the council would not be backsniped or have stumbling blocks put in its way. The council needed DAIA expertise, however, and would phase out official help over a three-year maximum period. He also believed that all moneys coming in should go through the council and the council should control permits.

Mr Wayne Connolly asked about what would happen to the houses and Mr Katter said that if the government appointed the council as trustees, they would own the houses. If the people wanted their own homes, maybe they could buy them from the council, suggested Mr Katter. They would then pay rent or rates plus house repayments.

Someone asked about pay and Cr Mick Connolly said they were 'on the verge of award wages: Welcome to Queensland'.

Mr Katter left at this point and the meeting continued with a number of questions including one about white staff. Cr Mick Connolly replied that the council wanted white police and teachers there. White police would never be phased out. There was nothing personal against staff but they had to trust Aborigines for a change.

The council had been a figurehead for too long in the opinion of Cr Mick Connolly. He said he would like to see a Yarrabah person on the Cairns Hospital Board, and Aboriginal police decently trained.

There was some controversy over how much power the council had in relation to the beer canteen. Mr Colin Neal asked, if the council were to lower their high prices at the beer canteen, would the manager approve it. The chairman, Cr Roy Gray, said that the council could not bring the prices down now. The people would have to wait for the new legislation.

Mr Percy Neal asked if the council was permitted to authorise 10.00 am–10.00 pm trading hours. Cr Mick Connolly said that when the new legislation came in, the council would have regular trading hours. (At the moment, it is illegal to trade more than four hours a day.)

Mrs Anna Palmer complained that the police searched cars of Aborigines coming into Yarrabah to see if they were carrying alcohol but they did not search cars with whites in them. (Regulation 13 under the Queensland Aborigines Act 1971–9 made it illegal for persons to bring alcohol onto the reserve or be in possession of it. Because of the short trading hours, the disallowance of take-aways and the fact that no wines or spirits are served in the canteen, the 'sly grog' trade flourishes on Yarrabah with beer, wine and spirits sold at exorbitant prices. European staff were, however, allowed to bring any kind of alcohol onto the reserves and drink it in their homes.) Cr Mick Connolly pledged the council would stamp out anomalies.

'It was sad', said Cr Mick Connolly, 'that the DAIA had not trained more Aborigines. They wanted us to cling to them all our life'. The community believes the reason for this has been to protect DAIA jobs. The council was looking at training programs, e.g. Community Employment Program (CEP).

Father Malcolm, the Aboriginal Church of England minister for Yarrabah, who had chaired the meeting, ended with a summary: 'We all want self-management, controlled by the council.'

This overview of the situation is geared toward the presentation and discussion of Aboriginal aspirations, so that the responses from Mr Katter are only touched upon.

G. Community Services (Aborigines) Bill 13 April 1984

On 13 April 1984, the Queensland Government rammed through the Community Services (Torres Strait) Bill and the Community Services (Aborigines) Bill after a record twenty-two hour sitting in which the government abandoned its own standing orders requiring new legislation to be on the table of the House for two days.[47]

---

[47] *The Cairns Post* 14 April 1984, p.1.

The House rose for winter recess at 8.40 am on 13 April but the six Liberal members left at midnight in what one described as a 'boycott of an exercise in futility'.[48]

The Community Services (Aborigines) Bill was presented for the first time at 10.30 pm on 12 April. A fiery debate over the Community Services (Torres Strait) Bill ensued from 9.00 pm on 12 April till 7.35 am on 13 April, when it was passed. The Community Services (Aborigines) Bill was passed one hour later following fifty minutes of debate on its eighty-four clauses after the government gagged the debate.

In introducing the legislation, Mr Katter said, 'This Bill reflects the Government's desire to unfetter Aboriginal and Islander people in formulating decisions which affect the development of their communities ... Education, hygienic lifestyles and provision of basic services all required a very high degree of control (in the past)'.

Mr Katter claimed that the Bills would give local government to the communities. 'However the legislation differed from local government legislation because of the problems of isolation and special funding.'[49]

The National Aboriginal Conference (NAC) Queensland chairman, Mr Steve Mam, reflected the opinion of the Yarrabah Council and most of the Yarrabah community when he said, 'Many of our people saw the legislation as a chance for this Government to right a lot of wrongs —instead they received a mirror of the old ways. It has been a complete deception'.[50]

Three Yarrabah councillors went to Brisbane to watch the passage of the legislation through the House. While in Brisbane ten out of the twelve councillors from the reserves signed a petition to have Mr Killoran removed from his position as under-secretary of the

---

[48] ibid.
[49] ibid.
[50] Ibid.

new Department of Community Services which will replace the DAIA. (Mr Killoran has been director for twenty-one years of the DAIA and its predecessor, the Department of Native Affairs.)[51]

The Yarrabah councillors arrived home from Brisbane crestfallen. Rather than seeing the new legislation as an unfettering of the chains binding Queensland Aboriginal communities, the chairman of Yarrabah, Mr Roy Gray, said that it was a name change but not a real change. The power was still in the hands of the department, not the Aboriginal council as they had been led to believe it would be.[52]

H. Attempt to Remove Executive Officer 17 April 1984

At a council meeting at Yarrabah on 17 April 1984, the chairman, Cr Roy Gray, read out a motion that the executive officer under the new legislation (i.e. the present manager on each community) be requested to stay for a three-month period only.[53] Under the new Act this position will exist for a three-year period unless an Aboriginal council requests a shorter or longer period. To shorten the period, an Order-in-Council is required. Under section 24 of the Act:

> (a) personnel and property of the Department shall not be utilised for the Council's purposes except with the Executive Officer's approval first had and obtained;
> (b) expenditure shall not be incurred or approved against moneys appropriated by Parliament and allocated to the use or benefit of the area for which the Council is established except with the Executive Officer's approval first had and obtained.

---

[51] Statement made by Alf Neal of Yarrabah Council at Yarrabah April 1984. Author's unpublished record.
[52] Author's unpublished record of interviews, April 1984.
[53] Yarrabah Council Meeting, Yarrabah, 17 April 1984. Minutes. Unpublished.

The manager was incensed at this proposal and threatened to take the property, personnel and finance of the department with him. He charged the council with irresponsibility and brandished the spectre of chaos before their eyes. The council wavered. The deputy chairman said that they needed the department for a period to ensure a smooth changeover. The motion was not put to the vote but was deferred.

I. Request for Commonwealth Takeover 17 April 1984

The council was so dissatisfied with the Community Services (Aborigines) Act that it passed the following resolution moved by Robert Smallwood and seconded by Roy Gray:

> That Yarrabah Council request the Federal Minister for Aboriginal Affairs Mr Holding to implement Federal Policy and take-over and fund Yarrabah reserve for the people of Yarrabah and implement self-management and the Minister's five principles regarding land rights and that the request be in the form of a telegram.[54]

J. Commonwealth Government Response 9 May 1984

Three weeks later, on 9 May, the Federal Minister for Aboriginal Affairs Mr Clyde Holding, replied by telegram to the Yarrabah Council. Here are extracts:

> ... As you will be aware, we have for some time been consulting Aboriginal people through the Steering Committee which I established last year to determine how they would wish to see the five principles relating to land rights translated into legislative action. The processes of consultation still required with the Aboriginal people and other interested parties are

---

[54] ibid.

such that it will not be possible to enact model land rights before 1985.

In the meantime the Commonwealth Government is concerned to ensure that the interests of the Aboriginal and Torres Strait Islander people in Queensland are fully protected.

I have sought an early meeting with the Queensland Minister for Aboriginal Affairs, Mr Katter, to discuss the situation at Yarrabah and other issues of concern in an endeavour to resolve them in an acceptable manner to the Aboriginal people.

I am also having the new legislation closely examined by the Government's legal advisors. The issues are complex and I wish to be sure that all aspects are properly examined.[55]

The real problem is that the federal government is calling elections before the end of 1984. Federal land rights legislation was promised for the 1984 August Budget sessions. However, the NAC have asked for more consultation time so that the federal government will not now introduce the legislation until after the election. The Aboriginal and Torres Strait Islanders Heritage (Interim Protection) Bill 1984 is now being presented to test some of the principles which will be embodied in the land rights legislation.

This response by the federal government has meant that Yarrabah feels left in the lurch with nowhere to turn for redress. The council feels forced by the federal government's attitude to work with the new

---

[55] Telegram from the Federal Minister for Aboriginal Affairs, Mr Clyde Holding, 9 May 1984. Unpublished, held by Yarrabah Council.

Queensland legislation under protest because there is no alternative they can see. This will be further discussed later.

K. Mr Katter s Response 19 April 1984

The minister launched a media attack on Roy Gray, saying that he was duped by the NAC. 'By the sounds of it Mr Gray is playing right into their [NAC] hands. I'm sorry he hasn't been clever enough to wake up to the fact he's being used as a puppet.'[56]

Bob Katter's response was much swifter than the federal government's. Two days after the telegram was sent to Canberra, he had a special meeting with the Yarrabah Council. Although I attended this meeting, Mr Katter requested that no comment be made to the media on the proceedings so I will limit myself to a discussion of the concerns brought up by the council in order to respect the council's and Mr Katter's wishes in this matter.

All I will say about Mr Katter is that he promised to work towards amendments of the legislation, said that he had been defeated on some points in the Bill and that on others he did not agree with the council's objections.[57]

The chairman, Mr Roy Gray, told *The Cairns Post* on 23 April 1984 that discussions with Mr Katter had been 'fruitful' and he said that the council still remained unhappy about the content of the recently passed Aboriginal and Islander legislation.

L. Council s Attitude to New Act 19 April 1984

The chairman, Cr Gray, said that the Community Services (Aborigines) Act was 'a name change, not a real change'. The council was worried that Mr Katter's approach was piecemeal. Deputy Chairman Mick Connolly wanted all the chairmen together to discuss the new legislation. (This meeting was held at Weipa on 24–25 May.)

---

[56] *The Cairns Post*, 19 April 1984, p.l.
[57] Yarrabah Council Meeting, Yarrabah 19 April 1984. Author's unpublished record.

Cr Alf Neal kept asking the question 'Why doesn't Yarrabah run its own affairs?' [58]

(1) Financial accountability

The council members were concerned about their personal liability to repay illegal expenditure. Section 29 of the Act says that the minister has to approve the budget of the council for non-trust funds which must be submitted each August in the form prescribed. Section 30 provides that the minister can sue the councillors in the name of the council for any expenditure of funds he did not approve or which was not provided for in the budget. The council members are jointly liable to repay this illegal expenditure.

Under the Local Government Act, a council must make and keep to a budget (s.25) but it does not have to be approved by a minister. The provision in the Community Services (Aborigines) Act for illegal expenditure is little different from the Local Government Act except that under the latter, only a ratepayer or creditor can take action, whereas under the Community Services (Aborigines) Act it is the minister.

(2) Under-Secretary's powers

The power of the under-secretary was a matter of great concern for the council, particularly that he has chairmanship, execution and control of the affairs of the Aboriginal Industries Board (AIB) and any business conducted by the board for five years (s.54(2) and s.58(4)). The council was upset that Mr Killoran would be retaining his position for five years which was longer than the three-year phasing-out period for the executive officer.

(3) Aboriginal Industries Board

The council felt that the new AIB to be set up was the old Aborigines Welfare Fund under a new name. Under the repealed

---

[58] ibid.

Aborigines Act, money from enterprises on reserves went into the Aborigines Welfare Fund administered by the department for the use of all the communities. The AIB will operate similarly (s.60). The council members are adamant, however, that 'resources should be used for the benefit of this community only'.

'What about development we don't want?' is a question that the council keeps asking. In all the consultation before the legislation, the council put the view that it should own the assets now owned by the department on Yarrabah and that it would make decisions as to what enterprises the council would run or what enterprises would be run by Yarrabah individuals on a private enterprise basis or by the Yarrabah Co-operative.

It is unacceptable to the council to have outsiders come in and set up enterprises on areas excised from the deed area for public purposes. But it is also unacceptable to the council to have the AIB own and run enterprises on Yarrabah. This would be its feeling whether or not the AIB was an all-Aboriginal elected body. However, the fact that the under-secretary is the chairman, and the AIB cannot have a meeting without him or his nominee (s.57) and that the Governor-in-Council will be appointing three (possibly Europeans) of the members of the AIB makes Aboriginal self-management hollow in the council's eyes.

Much to the council's dismay there is no guarantee that a Yarrabah person will be on the AIB. The communities will be grouped into four divisions—probably Gulf, Peninsula, Northern, and Southern—and the Aboriginal Co-ordinating Council which consists of all the chairmen of the communities (the old Aboriginal Advisory Council) will select one Aboriginal resident from each division to be on the AIB plus one Aboriginal resident from any trust area.

'We don't want the AIB', the chairman told Mr Katter.[59] The AIB has more power than the Aboriginal Co-ordinating Council because it will have a secretariat, administrative and technical staff (s.58) and

---

[59] ibid.

can carry on business, acquire and maintain plant, train Aborigines and raise loans (s.59).

The government still has overriding control, however. The minister may recommend to the Governor-in-Council that an administrator replace AIB members without specifying a reason. The administrator can run the AIB for a period of up to two years (s.63).

The possible setting up of the AIB was not discussed with the Yarrabah Council before the legislation was enacted. The Department of Community Services will gradually divest its assets to the AIB and the AIB can relinquish its assets over a period of time to Aboriginal councils or community residents on request from Aboriginal councils (s.64).

(4) Ancillary rights

Cr Robert Smallwood told the meeting, 'We want water rights, timber, quarrying, and foraging rights. Timber is basic to the economy of the reserve. Delete that and this reserve won't function'.[60] However these rights are not given in the legislation.

(5) Veto power

The veto powers residing with the minister and the under-secretary and the amount of ministerial discretion in the Act were also a matter of concern to the council. The ministry can veto council by-laws for example. Cr Smallwood said, 'I ask that we hold all the veto powers'.[61]

(6) Executive Officer

Cr Alf Neal said, 'Why doesn't Yarrabah take over now? Killoran and the department are still in control. We just can't work while they're here'.

---

[60] ibid.
[61] ibid.

The executive officer is not responsible to the Aboriginal council but to the under-secretary. The Governor-in-Council must approve an Aboriginal council's request to have the executive officer for less than three years (s.23). The purse-strings are held by the executive officer who has to approve expenditure and the use of departmental property or personnel by the Aboriginal council (s.24). The council cannot hire or fire white staff or get unsuitable departmental staff transferred out. This was one of the major things the council requested from the government before the legislation was enacted. Moreover, the Governor-in-Council can dissolve an Aboriginal council in his absolute discretion.

'If we don't get this set of things, we want the Commonwealth', said Cr Neal.[62]

M. Amendments Council Requested: 2, 4 and 9 May 1984

While waiting for the Commonwealth response which arrived by telegram on 9 May, the council held meetings on 2, 4 and 9 May to discuss amendments to the legislation it would like to see as well as other council business. The following letter cannot adequately convey the tone of dejection of the chairman of Yarrabah when he wrote to the State Minister for Aboriginal and Islander Affairs on 14 May, 1984:[63]

> I have set out below a summary of the final Amendments and would like to state by way of a foreword to the Amendments that Council is dissatisfied generally with the Bill and is particularly unhappy with the Provisions concerning the Aboriginal Industries Board. Nevertheless, Council is

---

[62] ibid.
[63] Letter from Cr Roy Gray, Chairman Yarrabah Council, to the State Minister for Aboriginal and Island Affairs, Mr. Bob Katter, 14 May 1984. Unpublished, held by Yarrabah Council.

prepared to work with the new legislation mainly because there seems to be little alternative but insist that the proposed Amendments to the Bill be adopted. Council will also request at a later date that the three-year term of office of the Executive Officer be reduced to an appropriate shorter term.

s.14 - Define what constitutes a 'community'. This is uncertain at present.

s.22 - Recommend a maximum period of 3 months between the date of dissolution of a Council and the date for fresh elections.

s.29 - Your Director has already stated in a letter reference 1A/1867 of 20th April, 1984 that Commonwealth Funds paid into Trust Funds will not be required to be included in budgets prepared for your approval under this section.

Recommended that you clarify whether the said 'Trust Funds' will be Trust Funds in terms of State Trust Fund Act.

s.33 - Recommended that this section be amended to specifically exclude 'Trust Funds' from Financial Returns required by this section.

s.41 - Recommended that you specify that extra Funds be provided to allow for performance of the various non-police functions listed.

s.42(3) - This does not spell out whether a Justice must disqualify himself from hearing a matter in which he has a personal interest by way of family ties. Recommended that this be clarified.

s.55(2) - This does not seem consistent with the provisions of s.23 (Executive Officer's appointment to run for 3 years). Recommend you clarify.

s.65 - Not acceptable to Council. Recommended that public roads be not excluded from Deed of Grant in Trust.

s.67 - The Reference in sub-section (b) to 'material comforts' is too vague - amend by including specifics. Amend also to cover rights of privacy for occupants of Trust Area houses.

s.77 - Final Amendment is:-
Sub-section (1) - delete 'by traditional means' substitute 'for traditional foods'.
Sub-section (2) - delete 'by traditional means' substitute 'for traditional purposes'.

N. Discussion of Amendments

(1) Torres Strait Islanders (s. 14)

What concerns the council about s.14 is that Aboriginal councils will have no jurisdiction over a community of Torres Strait Islanders within a trust area and there is no definition of what constitutes such a community or how it would be governed.

(2) Dissolution of Councils (s. 22)

The Governor-in-Council can dissolve an Aboriginal council in his absolute discretion and replace it with an administrator. There is no time limit during which fresh elections must be called (s.20-22).

(3) Trust funds (s.29)

There was quite a furore at Yarrabah and in DAA circles over the possibility that Commonwealth funds would also come under state government control by being required to be included in council budgets which will be subject to ministerial approval. For example, the Yarrabah Council members were worried that their budgeting for a project officer would not be approved. Commonwealth funds paid into trust funds will not, however, be affected as trust funds are excluded from these requirements.

(4) Financial accountability (s.33)

The Act requires the council to give monthly financial returns to the minister for three years and after that quarterly. This differs from the Local Government Act which provides for the town clerk to present internal financial returns to the council monthly and annually. The only information the government gets about the finances of local authorities is through the auditor-general's report to the treasurer.[64] The financial controls on Aboriginal councils are much tighter than those on local authorities. The council has not actually complained about this section. It has only recommended that 'trust funds' be excluded from the financial returns required under the section.

(5) Non-police functions (s.41)

An Aboriginal council may by its by-laws add various non-police functions to the role of Aboriginal police under the new Act (s.41), such as ambulance, fire-fighting, and emergency services. The Yarrabah Council recommended that extra funds be provided for this purpose.

---

[64] Local Government Act 1936-1983 (Qld), s.29(4).

(6) Under-Secretary (s.55(2))

As indicated, the council was concerned that the under-secretary was to hold office as chairman of the Aboriginal Industries Board for five years, while executive officers would be phased out in three years. The council has asked for clarification.

(7) Permits—visitors (ss.65,67)

Section 65(1) allows anyone to enter on and be in any public place, road, park or any place of business within an area if he or she is there for a lawful purpose. The council has stated that s.65 is not acceptable. Sub-section (2) basically says that any person is authorised to enter and be in any place at all on the community area if there for a lawful purpose as a guest of a community member. The council believes that it should have control over public roads. Councillors would like to keep a permit system, partly because they do not want a lot of tourists gawking at them and because they are worried it will open up Yarrabah for development. The council is not opposed to development but the councillors want to control it.

Groups of persons are authorised to stay temporarily in the area and s.67(1)(b) provides for people bringing religious instruction, material comforts, or medical aid. The council believes 'material comforts' is too vague and should be amended to be made more specific.

(8). Hunting and fishing (s.77)

Residents may hunt and fish by traditional means for their own consumption. The council wants 'traditional means' deleted and 'for traditional foods' substituted. Section 77(2) says residents may not sell marine products or fauna taken by traditional means. The council wants 'by traditional means' deleted and 'for traditional purposes' substituted.

D. New Regulations Discussed 14 May 1984

(1) Draft requested

The council met on 14 May to discuss recommendations for the regulations to accompany the Community Services (Aborigines) Act. It was decided that this was like groping in the dark and the council resolved to 'request that the Minister for Aboriginal and Torres Strait Island Affairs supply it with a draft copy of the new regulations for examination and further discussions by Council'.[65]

(2) Voting system

Most discussion was related to explanations given by the council's solicitor, Mr Greg McIntyre, on the implications of the new Act for the old regulations. Not all councillors were present when certain important decisions were made. However, 'it was generally agreed that the best method of voting would be an optional preferential points system with voting being compulsory with age being 18'. It was also resolved 'that Council retain the right to select its own Clerk'.[66]

(3) Eligibility of voters and candidates

The council had recommended to the Queensland Government on 19 March that only Aborigines be eligible to vote and stand as candidates for council elections. The feeling was the same at this meeting although the new Act says that membership of a community is not confined to Aborigines (s.66(1) (a)). This will probably mean that any non-Aborigines actually resident in trust areas will be eligible to vote for council. Staff and others residents in areas excised from the reserves/trust areas will be eligible to vote for local government councils.

---

[65] Yarrabah Council Meeting, Yarrabah, 14 May 1984, Minutes p.2.
[66] ibid.

(4) Assimilation

The council expressed dismay that the third part of the regulations-making power in the new Act referred to 'the development, assimilation, and integration of Aborigines' (s.82(3)). It was worried about what regulations might be included under the heading 'assimilation'.

P. Public Meeting 18 May 1984

The manager asked the council to call a public meeting to decide what recommendations to put to the state government on the hours of operation of the canteen (previously four hours daily), on the limit to be put on take-aways (previously not allowed), and on the question of staff wages. He said it would not be clear till the regulations were out whether the under-secretary would still be licensee or whether the council would hold the licence.

Since the Community Services (Aborigines) Act was passed on 13 April, there had been no public meeting at Yarrabah to explain the implications of the new Act and dissatisfaction had arisen in the community as a result. Few people seem to have known about the public meeting—only twenty-five residents attended at the start of the meeting—but those who did attend were incensed at the agenda. Their priority was not the operation of the beer canteen; they were concerned about who was going to run Yarrabah and how, and who owned the land. 'We don't want to discuss the pub. We want to discuss the land issue. We can't control anything without the land', said Mr Colin Neal of the Yarrabah Co-operative.[67]

A past chairman of Yarrabah Council Mr Percy Neal, who is now chairman of the Yarrabah Co-operative, made a number of points. He requested that the council do a survey on the effect of alcohol on Yarrabah residents and said that there had been an agreement at the last public meeting that the council approach the department to let its

---

[67] Public Meeting, Yarrabah, 18 May 1984. Author's unpublished record.

workers have half a day off with pay to attend public meetings. He said the council should not accept regulations unseen.

(1) Community request Commonwealth Government take-over

After three more residents arrived, the following motion was moved by Mr Percy Neal, seconded by Mr Stewart Harris and carried 28–0:

> We totally reject the new legislation that has been introduced because there have been broken promises in the past. The Premier said there would be full consultation at grass roots level. This has not been done. The way the Services legislation was pushed through is an insult to our intelligence. We totally reject it and ask for Federal intervention to apply to the whole reserve. We ask the Federal Government to assume the responsibilities given to it by the 1967 Referendum. [68]

A copy was sent to the Prime Minister Mr Bob Hawke, and the Federal Minister for Aboriginal Affairs Mr Clyde Holding.

The chairman felt that it was a bit pointless going through this exercise again. He said the council had already sent a similar telegram to the federal government and had been told that the government was not prepared to make any move till 1985. He felt there was really no alternative to working with the state legislation under protest. The community members, however, still wanted their input.

Q. Yarrabah Petition

After the public meeting, a petition was taken around the community and over 400 signatures (over 60 per cent of the adult population) had been received at the time of writing this report, and the petition is still circulating (May 1984).

---

[68] ibid.

To the Honourable Speaker and Members of the House of Representatives in Parliament assembled. The petition of the undersigned citizens of Australia respectfully showeth:

That the humble petitioners respectfully believe that the Federal Government has the power conferred on it by the 1967 Referendum to intervene on behalf of Aboriginal people in any conflict with any State or Territory Government. Your petitioners therefore pray:

That the Federal Government will accept its responsibility and use its powers under the Constitution to over-ride racist State legislation such as was recently introduced into the Queensland Government, and particularly to provide Land Rights with freehold title, for the Residents of the Yarrabah Community and that in addition the Government fulfil its stated policy of self-determination and self-management for Aboriginal people, by funding all housing, health, education, legal, employment strategy, and welfare matters concerning Aboriginal people directly through Aboriginal community based, community controlled organisations such as a Corporate Body, whose membership would comprise the Aboriginal residents of the Yarrabah Community, who would elect a Council to manage the land and waters, mining, timber, tourism and fishing as well as the previously mentioned organisations, thus enabling the elected Council to control all matters necessary to enable the Yarrabah Community to function in the manner which the members of the Yarrabah Community might desire from time to time.

So that these aims may be accomplished, we therefore call upon the Federal Government to use its powers of acquisition to take over the Yarrabah land for the Yarrabah residents. By this petition we totally reject the Queensland Legislation and call upon the Manager of Yarrabah to resign and forthwith leave our land.

And your petitioners as in duty bound will ever pray: ...[69]

A. Comparison of the Act with Yarrabah s Proposals of 19 March 1984

(1) Council

The size of the council, and eligibility to vote and stand for elections will be covered in the new regulations which had not been sighted by any Aboriginal group at the time of writing this report. The term of office of the council is three years as requested.

(2) Permits—residency

The council no longer has power to grant permits of residency as requested but under s.68 may make by-laws consistent with ss.65-67 of the Act authorising or excluding a class of persons specified from entering or residing in the area. This leaves little room to manoeuvre because s.66 says that people who are authorised to reside in a trust area are Aborigines or other people who, in either case, are members of the resident community and people discharging a function under this Act or any other Act requiring their presence in the area.

'A member of the community resident in an area' is a bit vague in the council's opinion. In their submission of 19 March 1984, council members had requested power over public servants which they do not have in this Act:

---

[69] Yarrabah's Community petition, May 1984. Unpublished, copy held by author.

Council will require public servants posted to Yarrabah to be granted permits to live at Yarrabah; Council will grant such permits in the first instance for three months only; at the expiry of three months, any public servant considered to be an undesirable resident will be issued a Notice to Show Cause why his or her Permit to Reside at Yarrabah should not be revoked.[70]

(3) Manager and Council

There are significant departures from the Local Government Act which are discussed in the next section of this report. The council requested at its March meeting that it 'have the full powers of a normal Town Council'.

Yarrabah's representative in the Queensland Parliament, Mr Keith De Lacy, the member for Cairns, told parliament on 12 April 1984 in debate on the Bill:

> When I visit Yarrabah I'm confronted with the absurd situation in which there are two administrations—the DAIA, which has the real power, spends most of the money and makes the decisions on road-building, schools and other matters, and the Community Council which has been elected by the people but cannot make decisions. One group does not know what the other group is doing. The two groups do not communicate very well and there is no friendship between them.[71]

---

[70] Yarrabah Council Meeting, Yarrabah, 19 March 1984, *Minutes*, p.2.
[71] Queensland, Legislative Assembly, *Hansard*, 12 April 1984, vol.294, p.2890.

Commonwealth funds have given the council some independence, but the member's observation is basically true. Although the school is run by the Queensland Education Department, the DAIA has significant policy input.

The council had hoped the new Act would create one administration, with the council seconding selected departmental staff for a period of up to three years to help it carry out local government functions. The council wanted the executive officer to be employed by the council in the role of a shire clerk.

The line of control is, however, really no different from before: under-secretary to executive officer to council. The council still has 'Big Brother' to contend with. Members of the Yarrabah Council experience difficulty in their relations with the manager/executive officer. At both public meetings held at Yarrabah on 8 April and 18 May, the manager raised his voice, jumped up and advanced towards Aboriginals he disagreed with, pointing an accusing finger at them in an intimidating manner. On 8 April he called a community member and the deputy chairman liars, although he later retracted his accusation about the community member when the Co-operative chairman pressed him for an apology.[72]

(4) Community Courts

The council requested 'that there be constituted at Yarrabah a Magistrates Court comprising two or more Aboriginal Justices of the Peace'.[73] The Act however provides that there shall be two courts at Yarrabah: an Aboriginal court and a magistrates court. The Aboriginal court may hear charges concerning breaches of the council's by-laws, matters committed to its jurisdiction by the regulations, and disputes that are not breaches of by-laws or Commonwealth or state law. Previously, only Aborigines could be tried but now non-Aboriginal

---

[72] Yarrabah Council Public Meeting, Yarrabah, 8 April 1984. Author's unpublished record.

[73] Yarrabah Council Meeting, Yarrabah, 19 March 1984, *Minutes*, p.2.

residents are under the Aboriginal court's jurisdiction. Residents cannot elect to have their cases heard in a magistrates court. However, s.45 says that any person aggrieved by his/her conviction in an Aboriginal court will have the same right of appeal as if convicted in a magistrates court, which is an improvement.

The Bill creates two classes of persons and is discriminatory because the jurisdiction of the Aboriginal court does not extend to public servants who are charged in a magistrates court for by-law infringements. It is interesting that the distinction is no longer between Aborigines and non-Aborigines but between residents (close to 100 per cent Aboriginal) and public servants (close to 100 per cent European).

Another council request was that court fines be remitted to the Yarrabah Community Fund and that these moneys not be paid into consolidated revenue. This is not covered in the Act.[74]

(5) Police

Although the council requested that Aboriginal police 'training be up-graded to State Police standards within a specially devised program for Aboriginals',[75] there is no statutory requirement for such training and the Act does not foreshadow providing regulations for the training of Aboriginal police. The Yarrabah Council will probably have to organise such training itself and seek Commonwealth Government funding, since Aboriginal police become a council responsibility under the Community Services (Aborigines) Act. The council can appoint as many Aboriginal police as it likes with the minister's approval (s.39) and must provide them with a uniform and 'such other marks of authority as it thinks fit'. In order to achieve better integration with the state police it would be more appropriate for Aboriginal police to have their appointment by councils confirmed

---

[74] ibid.
[75] ibid.

by the police minister, rather than the minister responsible for the Community Services (Aborigines) Act.

(6) Canteen and alcohol

This is dealt with in the regulations. From the information provided by the manager at the public meeting on 18 May, the regulations will set down the maximum number of hours the beer canteen can be open daily and the council can only choose to operate fewer hours, and to vary the times of operating. This is less power than requested, which was to decide the hours of operation. It is uncertain whether the council will be the licensee as requested, or whether the canteen will be able to sell any type of liquor other than beer despite the application of the council.

It is hardly self-management when under s.76 of the Act an Aboriginal council needs the permission of the under-secretary to establish a beer canteen and the under-secretary can close it down if he thinks it is causing 'breaches of the peace', or is 'detrimental to the health and well-being' of residents or 'a source of danger to the life and safety' of residents, or if take home supplies exceed council by-law limits. At least in this instance some reasons are specified, vague though some of them are. Often the Act leaves veto or terminating powers up to the 'absolute discretion' of the minister or under-secretary. The Liquor Act does not apply except for section 81 which covers ejection of disorderly persons.

(7) Advisory Council

This has been retained as council requested and renamed the Aboriginal Co-ordinating Council. It consists of the chairmen of all the Aboriginal communities as before, but will now be incorporated, able to sue and hold property which is an improvement. It still has only advisory powers and no secretariat or independent funding. (The council requested funding for a secretariat from the Commonwealth Government.) But it can appoint five out of the nine people on the

Aboriginal Industries Board (ss.46-53). No provision has been made for the ACC to 'appoint sub committees to investigate special issues' as submitted by Yarrabah Council.

(8) Aboriginal and Islanders Commission

The commission was an advisory body appointed by the Queensland Government and consisted of one community Aborigine, one urban Aborigine, one Torres Strait Islander and one South Sea Islander.

The Aboriginal and Islanders Commission has been abolished by virtue of being left out of the Services Legislation. Yarrabah's proposal of 9 June 1983 had suggested this.

Yarrabah suggested separate legislation for Aborigines not living on communities. (My impression is that Cairns Aborigines do not want such legislation unless the government gives land rights over unalienated Crown land, sacred sites and areas of traditional significance not on reserves.)

(9) Miscellaneous

Yarrabah Aborigines continue to have the right to hunt and fish on the community in accordance with council wishes. But as indicated above the council has proposed amendments to make the relevant provision of the Act more satisfactory.

(10) Additional

(a) Disqualification of Councillors

This is not covered in the Act but is dealt with in the regulations.

(b) Management of property

The council's resolution 'that the special provisions of the existing State Act regarding management of the property of

Aboriginal people be abolished and that in future, management of property should be handled by the Yarrabah Magistrates Court' was not put into effect.[76] The under-secretary will continue to manage the property of Aborigines managed by the director under the old Act (s.73). This has not been compulsory for many years.

(c) Grants-in-aid

Despite a request that grants-in-aid powers be transferred to the council, these powers to assist Aborigines in need remain with the under-secretary (s.71).

(d) Welfare fund

The council had hoped that the centralised Aborigines Welfare Fund controlled by the department would be abolished and its assets distributed to community councils, because most of the income from the communities has gone into this fund over the years (with the notable exception of beer canteen income).

This meant to the council 'an automatic takeover of all fixed assets, e.g. sawmill, store etc. plus any monies still held after the fund has been audited and the books closed off'. However, s.5(8) states that the Aborigines Welfare Fund will continue and be maintained by the under-secretary.

(e) Other assets

The council requested 'that on implementation of the new Act, all other buildings and items of plant presently owned by DAIA at Yarrabah be handed over to it', but the Act provides that the department will continue to own property in the communities. My impression is that it is intended that some

---

[76] ibid., p.3.

property will be gradually handed over to the council, to individual residents or to the AIB, the last in turn gradually handing it over to local control. It is expected that the federally funded Aboriginal Development Commission will help finance such ventures.

V.
YARRABAH, HUMAN RIGHTS AND SELF-MANAGEMENT.

A. Comparison with Local Government Act

Some form of local government has been provided for in the Community Services (Aborigines) Act but there are significant departures from both the Local Government Act and the Local Government (Aboriginal Lands) Act 1978 which applies to the former Aboriginal reserves of Aurukun and Mornington Island.

I. Not responsible to Local Government Minister

Firstly, Aurukun and Mornington Island, like other local authorities, are responsible to the Minister for Local Government not to the Minister for Aboriginal and Island Affairs. Some Yarrabah Aborigines suspect that responsibility has not been passed to the Minister for Local Government, not to serve the interests of Aborigines, but rather to preserve the jobs of departmental officers. DAIA staff could have been seconded to Aboriginal councils as proposed by the Yarrabah Council and gradually transferred to other government departments, unless they came to an arrangement with councils to stay on as employees.

2. Financial accountability

Under s.29 of the Community Services (Aborigines) Act, the minister has to approve the budget of Aboriginal councils submitted in August each year in the form prescribed. All non-Aboriginal councils, as well as the Aurukun and Mornington Island Councils, simply have to have their budget available for public inspection.[77]

The minister can sue councillors in the name of the council for any expenditure of funds he did not approve or which were not provided for in their budget. They are jointly liable to repay this illegal expenditure (s.30). Under the Local Government Act, only electors or creditors of the council can sue for illegal expenditure.

Much more ministerial discretion is operative in the Community Services (Aborigines) Act where the minister prescribes which accounts are to be kept. Accounts required are set out by the regulations under the Local Government Act (s.29(1)).

Frank Brennan, in his Consultation Document No. 8 says:

> Whereas the Under-Secretary or any person authorised by him is empowered to enter premises to inspect records and to make copies, there is requirement for ordinary Councils to comply with any summons made by the auditor for the production of records etc. (s.29(5)(v) Local Government Act). There is no general power of entry given an auditor of an ordinary Council even if it be the subject of a special audit ordered by the Minister (s.29(10) Local Government Act). [An Aboriginal Council is to be audited] as if the Council were a department of government of Queensland (s.32(2)).[78]

Aboriginal councils are required to give monthly financial returns to the minister for three years and after that quarterly (s.33(1)). This differs materially from the Local Government Act where the

---

[77] Local Government Act 1936-1983 (Qld), s.25

[78] Frank Brennan S.J. Consultation documents on services legislation for Aborigines and Torres Strait Islanders in Queensland, No.8, 12 April 1984, p.6. Unpublished, held by Qld Catholic Bishops.

town clerk gives a monthly report to the council. Similarly, s.33(2) provides for Aboriginal councils to give annual statements to the minister whereas the Local Government Act requires the town clerk to give annual statements to the council. The government gets feedback on ordinary councils through audit procedures.

3. Not Local Government

'Without amendment bringing them into line with similar provisions of the Local Government Act, [these clauses] are not the stuff of self-management nor even of responsible local government', said Frank Brennan. 'These provisions effect such a substantial shift in financial responsibility from the elected Council to the Minister and the Under-Secretary as to render the grant of local government powers subject to the overriding discretion of the Minister and the Under-Secretary. I cannot agree with the Minister's proposition that these local government provisions "are bringing these communities into line with the rest of the State". In many instances, it is "as if the Council were a department of government of Queensland".'[79]

4. Elections

The State Electoral Office runs local government elections but there is no mention in the Community Services (Aborigines) Act of it running Aboriginal council elections, although this was requested by the fourteenth meeting of the Aboriginal Advisory Council.[80] In the past there has been too much DAIA interference in council elections. The Local Government Act does not apply to Aboriginal council elections. Although s.18 requires a voters' roll to be kept, the regulations under the Community Services (Aborigines) Act can override LGA provisions. The Act does not indicate who the returning officer will be, and this will probably be covered in the regulations.

---

[79] ibid., p.7.
[80] Aboriginal Advisory Council, 14th Meeting, Brisbane, 4-5 August 1981. Minutes, p.7. Unpublished held by Dept. of Community Services (Qld), Brisbane.

B. Comparison with Human Rights Legislation and Conventions

An examination will be made to see if the Community Services (Aborigines) Act is in contravention of human rights as set out in the Racial Discrimination Act 1975, Aboriginal and Torres Strait Islanders (Queensland Discriminatory Laws) Act 1975, and international instruments relating to human rights and freedoms—the *International Convention on the Elimination of All Forms of Racial Discrimination* (the Convention) and the *International Covenant on Civil and Political Rights* (the Covenant).

I. Political rights

(a) Self-determination

The *United Nations Charter*, the *International Covenant on Civil and Political Rights* and the *International Covenant on Economic, Social and Cultural Rights* all assert the right of self-determination which is fundamental in international law. Article 1 of each Covenant is the same.

Article 1.1 asserts, 'All peoples have the right of self-determination. By virtue of that right they freely determine their political status and freely pursue their economic, social and cultural development'.

Professor of Law at the University of NSW, Garth Nettheim, in an analysis of the Community Services Bills says:

> Self-determination within the international provisions includes a right of a people to choose a separate national identity, but they also have the right to choose complete assimilation with other peoples or to choose among various other options between the two extremes. In the absence of any treaty, Aboriginal and Torres Strait Island peoples have not yet engaged in any act of choice in the matter. Australian federal governments appear unwilling to contemplate separate

nationhood for Aboriginal and Island peoples. But they do seem willing to accept some measure of community autonomy for established communities. The former Fraser Government's phrase 'self-management' seemed to contemplate the right of communities to make important decisions concerning their communities independently of the influence of governments and government officials.[81]

When Yarrabah and some other Queensland reserves petitioned the federal government under the Aboriginal and Torres Strait Islanders (Queensland Reserves and Communities Self-Management) Act 1978, the federal government did not respond.

The Hawke government seems to be similarly cautious about using the term 'self-determination' and to prefer to use the term 'self-management'. Queensland reserves have not made requests to the Hawke government under the federal self-management legislation because they have been promised national land rights legislation.

This report demonstrates that the Community Services (Aborigines) Act does not provide for self-determination. Over 60 per cent of the adults at Yarrabah have signed a petition rejecting this legislation and asking for federal intervention to ensure Yarrabah's right to self-determination.

(b) Participation in elections

'Political rights, in particular the rights to participate in elections—to vote and to stand for election—on the basis of universal and equal suffrage, to take part in the government as well as in the conduct of public affairs at any level and to have equal access to public service' is ensured by Article 5(c) of the Convention. Some Yarrabah residents are concerned that under s.18 of the Community Services

---

[81] Garth Nettheim, Community Services (Torres Strait) Bill 1984 and Community Services (Aborigines) Bill 1984. Unpublished, held by Aboriginal Law Research Unit (Victoria) 27 April 1984, p.5.

(Aborigines) Act, they will be struck off the roll and be ineligible to vote for or stand for Mulgrave Shire Council elections if they are on the voters' roll for Yarrabah Council elections.

Aborigines on northern communities suspect that s.18 is designed to prevent an increase in the number of black councillors on local government shires. The reserves/trust areas constitute large black voting blocks in these areas.

There are at present two Aborigines from Doomadgee on the Burke Shire Council and one from Kowanyama on the Carpentaria Shire Council. One of the present Yarrabah councillors stood for the Cairns City Council elections a few years ago while resident in Cairns, and polled favourably. Under the Community Services (Aborigines) Act, Aborigines will have to choose which voters' roll they want to be on. If Aboriginal councils had the same powers as other councils, there would be no quarrel with this disenfranchisement but they do not at this point constitute true local authorities.

Robert Smallwood, a Yarrabah councillor, made this complaint to the Human Rights Commission on 10 May 1984: 'The Queensland government intends to introduce a legislation which will prevent me as an Aboriginal resident of Yarrabah from having the right to vote in local government elections. Instead I can only vote for the Yarrabah Council, which is not the same.'[82]

The Cairns Consultative Committee on Community Relations, in forwarding this complaint on 23 May 1984, wrote:

> This Committee supports Mr Smallwood's formal complaint and requests the Commission to take immediate action with regard to sections of the proposed legislation which contravene existing Federal legislation. It is appreciated that

---

[82] Complaint made to Human Rights Commission by Mr Robert Smallwood, a Yarrabah Councillor of Yarrabah on 10 May 1984, p.1–2. Unpublished, held by Cairns Consultative Committee on Community Relations.

the Federal Government has the power to override State legislation but it seems provocative that a legislation should be proposed by the State which is oblivious to existing Federal Law.[83]

Mr Smallwood's view on voting rights is a minority one on the Yarrabah Council for reasons explained below. However, there is a body of opinion within the community which supports him on this issue.

Mr Smallwood has authorised the publication of the details of his complaint for the purposes of this report.

The Yarrabah Council does not see any advantage to Yarrabah residents in voting for Mulgrave Shire elections and approves s.18 because it is worried that the nearby Mulgrave Shire Council might decide that it needs to look after the welfare of its constituents in Yarrabah and start imposing building and other regulations on the community which it may not be able to meet (see section V B 4(a) of this report on housing problems). Previously, the Mulgrave Shire Council has adopted a low profile (except to help Yarrabah get an access road and employ Yarrabah Aborigines on road works) because Yarrabah was managed by the Queensland Government directly. Legal opinion is that the Community Services (Aborigines) Act, including s.18, will make little difference and that the council's fears are unfounded. Also, until the Yarrabah Council actually receives all deed of grant in trust under Queensland's Aboriginal land legislation (DOGIT) then any complaints by Mulgrave Shire Council would be directed to the Department of Community Services as the land owner.

The Chairman of the Mulgrave Shire Council, Cr Tom Pyne, has given the writer a verbal assurance that Mulgrave Shire Council regulations do not apply at Yarrabah (which has to abide by state government regulations) and the Mulgrave Shire Council will not be

---

[83] ibid.

undertaking any inspections at Yarrabah but believed Yarrabah should be self-managing. He is prepared to put this in writing to the Yarrabah Council.

Another concern of the council is that under the Community Services (Aborigines) Act (s.66) non-Aborigines can be residents of Yarrabah and therefore will be able to vote for council elections and stand for positions on the council unless the regulations find a way around it. The council does not want this because they have suffered from so much white paternalism in the past. They are afraid that if Aborigines can vote and stand for both Yarrabah Council and Mulgrave Shire Council then non-Aborigines will demand the same.

One way the regulations might get around this is that under DOGIT public servants living on Yarrabah will be living on land excised from the community and therefore will not be subject to council by-laws so a case could be made that they should not vote for Yarrabah Council.[84] They would then vote for the Mulgrave Shire Council only (which is the present situation). Non-Aborigines, particularly those who are not public servants, who are married to or living with Aborigines on land not excised from the community will present another problem. In other words, there is a tension between self-determination and human rights on the voting issue.

2. Civil rights

(a) Freedom of movement

'The right to freedom of movement and residence within the border of the State' is set out in the Convention (Article 5(d)(i)).[85] The Community Services (Aborigines) Act is an improvement over

---

[84] See discussion of Land Act 1962-1983 (Qld), s.344c, in part VI. B.2 (a) (i) and part VI.D.11 of this report.

[85] Extensively discussed in parts IV.N.6 and IV.R.2 of this report.

previous legislation which required permits for visits to and residency in Yarrabah. This caused problems for Aborigines who were out of favour with the council or, before federal overriding legislation in 1975, the DAIA. On other communities, there are complaints that managers still intimidate councils over permits.

There is a conflict of interests here between human rights and self-management because the Yarrabah Council would like to retain the permit system to ensure privacy and protect the land from incursion. Some Europeans maintain that Aborigines do not need a permit these days to visit or live in Cairns, so why should Europeans require one to visit or live in Yarrabah? What the Yarrabah Council would like to see is private property rights over Yarrabah vested in the Yarrabah community. The council believes it should have the power to preserve the integrity of the community through the permit system which could be compared to the passport system between sovereign states. Until the by-laws are drawn up by the Yarrabah Council, we do not know what class of persons might be excluded from the community but the by-laws will have to be in accordance with the Act.

Another human rights concern is that there is no right of appeal for persons excluded from the community. Persons excluded from Aurukun and Mornington Island have a right of appeal.[86]

(b) Right to inherit

Article 5(d)(vi) of the Convention guarantees the right to inherit. However, s.75 of the Community Services (Aborigines) Act provides that if Aborigines die without appointing an executor or if they are missing, the under-secretary determines who succeeds to an estate or if anybody does. If the under-secretary decides no one is entitled to inherit the estate, part of it will vest in the under-secretary who will use it for grant-of-aid money to Aborigines generally.

---

[86] Community Services (Aborigines) Act 1984 (Qld) s.69 and Local Government (Aboriginal Lands) Act 1978 (Qld), s.27 (2).

(c) Other civil rights

Rights to nationality, marriage and choice of spouse, to freedom of thought, conscience and religion, to freedom of opinion and expression, and freedom of peaceful assembly and association referred to in Article 5 of the Convention are not restricted by the Community Services (Aborigines) Act. It remains to be seen what the regulations and by-laws will produce, and whether the spirit of the law and its administration will ensure these rights.

3. Economic rights

(a) Equal pay

Article 5(e)(i) of the Convention establishes 'the rights to work, to *free* choice of employment, to just and favourable conditions of work, to protection against unemployment, to equal pay for equal work, to just and favourable remuneration'.

Although it is illegal under Commonwealth law—under both the Racial Discrimination Act and the Aboriginal and Torres Strait Islanders (Queensland Discriminatory Laws) Act 1975—the Queensland Government through the DAIA are still paying under-award wages to reserve Aborigines. The Industrial Court of Queensland declared in 1979 (after Yarrabah Aborigine, Arnold Murgha, put his case) that the State Building Trades Award applied in Aboriginal reserves.[87] This means that all State Awards apply on Aboriginal communities.

In 1980, DAIA increased wages to the guaranteed minimum wage. In recent years, Commonwealth funds have enabled councils and co-operatives to employ their own workers, e.g. Commonwealth Employment Program (CEP) schemes under which award wages are paid. A project presently in progress at Yarrabah necessitated the

---

[87] Australian Workers' Union of Employees (Qld) v. Director of Department of Aboriginal & Islanders Advancement (1979) 101 Q. Gov. Indus. Gaz., p.133. (Q. Indus. Ct).

council hiring DAIA machinery. Friction has been caused because council labourers receive $250 a week, while the DAIA machinery operators used on the project are being paid $212 a week by DAIA despite their skills. DAIA machine operators threatened to go on strike if the council did not top up their wages. The manager passed the problem onto the council, which ended up agreeing to employ DAIA workers for the duration of the project.

The Community Services (Aborigines) Act makes no pronouncement about award wages, nor do the regulations foreshadow anything about wages for black departmental workers. A number of councillors wondered whether some seventeen black DAIA workers (about three from each gang) were dismissed so that the Department of Community Services could begin on 31 May with a reduced workforce so that award wages could be paid, with the wages bill maintained at the same level. (Some of the seventeen workers were subsequently re-instated.)

The reason for this surmise is that arguments over recent years for the payment of under-award wages have been that workers would have to be sacked to keep the wages bill within budget. Arguments prior to that were that Aborigines were slow workers or were training, even when in fact no training was being given.

Rates of pay have only been one aspect of the problem. I am told by Yarrabah residents that in the past sick leave, holiday pay, long service pay and compensation have been problems, although I did not have time to research cases. The present situation is that some of the sacked workers had been working for the DAIA for over ten years and did not receive long service entitlements. They should have received pro rata payments. The council's solicitor is acting on their behalf in this matter.

(b) Joining trade unions

'The right to form and join trade unions' is established in Article 5(e)(ii) of the Convention and s.14 of the Racial Discrimination Act.

Nothing in the old or new legislation prohibits Yarrabah Aborigines from joining trade unions. However, today, as far as I know, not one Yarrabah resident is a member of a trade union.

Here it is necessary to understand that it is not just legislation we are talking about, but also administration. The whole ethos of the reserve system has been one of a 'captive' environment where, if Aborigines buck against the system, they get penalised by loss of jobs, going to the bottom of housing lists, police harassment etc. (Housing and police harassment will be dealt with later.) Previous councils (except for Percy Neal's council) have generally been more susceptible to the influence of managers who appear to have seen trade unions as a threat and the permit system as an effective psychological deterrent to trade union organisers.

Despite this, Arnold Murgha became a member of the Australian Workers Union (AWU), which took his case to the Queensland Industrial Court. As mentioned above, a decision favourable to award wages was reached in 1979. More Yarrabah workers joined the AWU and were promptly sacked, although with pressure from the union they were reinstated. Because of the non-payment of award wages and little follow-up by the AWU, confidence in the AWU was sapped.

(c) Control of resources

Article 1.2 of the Covenant states: 'All peoples may, for their own ends, freely dispose of their natural wealth and resources without prejudice to any obligations arising out of international economic co-operation, based upon the principle of mutual benefit, and international law. In no case may a people be deprived of its own means of subsistence.'

The Yarrabah Council is particularly sensitive on this point. It believes that the AIB and the Aborigines Welfare Fund constitute infringements of their human rights to control their own resources and derive income from their own resources.

As Cr Robert Smallwood said on 19 April, 'We want water rights, timber, quarrying and foraging rights. Timber is basic to the economy of the reserve. Delete that and this reserve won't function'.[88]

(d) Financial accountability

The definition of what constitutes racial discrimination is set out in Article 1.1 of the Convention and is embodied in section 9(1) of the Racial Discrimination Act.

> It is unlawful for a person to do any act involving a distinction, exclusion, restriction or preference based on race, colour, descent or national or ethnic origin which has the purpose or effect of nullifying or impairing the recognition, enjoyment or exercise, on an equal footing, of any human right or fundamental freedom in the political, economic, social, cultural or any other field of public life.

The provisions relating to financial oversight of the Yarrabah Council or other Aboriginal councils are discriminatory in that they are not applied to town and shire councils (including Aurukun and Mornington Island). The effect is to severely disadvantage Aboriginal councils. Aboriginal councils do not have the equality before the law guaranteed in the Racial Discrimination Act, 5.10(1):

> If by reason of, or a provision of, a law of Australia or of a State or Territory, persons of a particular race, colour or national or ethnic origin do not enjoy a right that is enjoyed by persons of another race, colour or national or ethnic origin, or enjoy a right to a more limited extent than persons of another race, colour or national or ethnic origin, then, notwithstanding anything in that law, persons of the first-mentioned race,

---

[88] Yarrabah Council Meeting, Yarrabah, 19 April 1984. Author's unpublished record.

colour, or national or ethnic origin shall, by force of this section, enjoy that right to the same extent as persons of that other race, colour or national or ethnic origin.

4. Social and cultural rights

(a) Right to housing

Section 5(e)(iii) of the Convention sets out this basic right. However, a joint ADC/DAA Aboriginal Housing and Accommodation Needs Survey in September 1983 assessed the housing situation at Yarrabah to be seventy houses in good condition, sixty houses and four duplexes in fair condition (routine repairs needed), thirty houses in poor condition (major repairs required) and in bad condition (replacement required) twenty houses, thirty pensioner units and 600 shelters.[89]

To rectify this poor housing situation, the ADC/DAA survey recommended the building of 120 houses, twenty pensioner units and two thirty-bed hostels.

In the light of this, it is interesting that under the Community Services (Aborigines) Act housing will be the responsibility of the Aboriginal council instead of the department. In fact, I heard a comment at a Yarrabah Council meeting break to the effect of 'now we know why DAIA didn't repair the houses. They knew they were going to give them to the council'. At the public meeting on 8 April, the minister said there would be no sudden withdrawal of finances. It would happen over a ten-year period.[90]

This is a matter of concern when income levels indicate that many Yarrabah families are in need of public housing assistance (state

---

[89] *Aboriginal Housing and Accommodation Needs Survey, September 1983.* Jointly conducted by the Aboriginal Development Commission Cairns and the Commonwealth Department of Aboriginal Affairs Cairns. Unpublished, held by these departments.

[90] Yarrabah Public Meeting, Yarrabah 8 April 1984. Author's unpublished record.

and/or Commonwealth), and will be for years to come. The Cairns Commonwealth Employment Service (CES) has not kept separate statistics for Aborigines since 1981 but its unofficial estimate is that two-thirds of the Yarrabah workforce (about 66%) are unemployed. Coupled with under-payment of award wages for DAIA workers and probably Department of Community Service workers, the picture is somewhat dismal.

Basic human rights will continue to be denied even though self-management is achieved in the housing area if there is no adequate resources back-up from government to meet the housing needs of the Yarrabah community.

(b) Right to privacy

The right to privacy in one's home is guaranteed by the Aboriginal and Torres Strait Islanders (Queensland Discriminatory Laws) Act 1975, s.8. However, this section and most other sections will no longer have effect if Aboriginal reserves in Queensland are degazetted, which will occur as the Deeds of Grant in Trust are made to councils.

Nevertheless, Aborigines on 'trust areas', as reserves like Yarrabah will be called, are entitled by s.9 of the Racial Discrimination Act to the same privileges as anybody else, e.g. the right to privacy in their dwellings. Also Article 17 of the Covenant covers the right to privacy.

In his Second Reading Speech on the Community Services (Aborigines) Bill, Mr Katter foreshadowed a possible amendment to the Deed of Grant legislation enabling separate titles to be held by householders, in which case they would have the same rights of exclusion and privacy as the Crown and other property holders.[91]

---

[91] Queensland, Legislative Assembly, *Hansard*, 12 April 1984, vol.294. (The Minister's Second Reading Speech on the Community Services (Aborigines) Bill).

If there is not such an amendment, then the council as trustee of the reserve/trust area would lease land to householders, in which case the householders would only have the same right of exclusion as does the council.

Yarrabah Council's solicitor, Greg McIntyre, writes:

> On a broad reading of the legislation, any member of the Community or resident discharging a statutory function could request any person to enter any part of a trust, whether it was the household of another person or not. It may be possible to limit this provision by means of by-laws. However ... such a limitation may be regarded as inconsistent with the right to enter on request contained in clause 65(2) and therefore outside the power to make exclusionary by-laws, contained in clause 68(6).[92]

An amendment may be required either to the Aboriginal and Torres Strait Islanders (Queensland Discriminatory Laws) Act or the Community Services (Aborigines) Act to ensure privacy of householders.

(c) Rights to medical care and education

Articles 5(e)(iv) and (v) of the Convention guarantee 'the right to public health, medical care, social security and social services; and the right to education and training'.

Health and education services are not dealt with by the Community Services (Aborigines) Act. Training will be covered in Part 4 of the regulations. One can only surmise that health care and education will continue in much the same way, education having been recently handed over by the DAIA to the Education Department, and

---

[92] Greg McIntyre, Community services legislation: the right of entry and land rights, p.9. Unpublished, held by author.

health care being shared by the new Department of Community Services and the Health Department through the Cairns Hospital Board and the State Aboriginal Health Program.

The right to self-determination set down in the Covenant supports the Yarrabah Council's desire to have more control in the health care of its community. In response to a query of mine on 2 May 1984, I received the following reply from the council:

> The Council believes the Community is reasonably satisfied with the health services at Yarrabah provided through the Hospital. However the Council would prefer to employ its own team of Aboriginal health field workers rather than the Aboriginal Health Program. The Council would like to include an ambulance driver in its team of health field workers.[93]

The Human Rights Commission is investigating a long-standing complaint from the Yarrabah Council that the community has been discriminated against in the unequal provision of educational facilities by the Queensland Government which has not provided covered walkways and a covered lunch area for the high school students to protect them from tropical summer rains and heat.

(d) Right to enjoy own culture

Article 27 of the Covenant states:

> In those States in which ethnic, religious or linguistic minorities exist, persons belonging to such minorities shall not be denied the right, in community with the other members of their group, to enjoy their own culture, to profess and practice their own religion, or to use their own language.

---

[93] Statement from Yarrabah Council to author, 2 May, 1984. Unpublished, held by author, and Yarrabah Council.

There is some degree of recognition of Aboriginal culture in the Community Services (Aborigines) Act. Section 25(1) charges the Aboriginal councils with 'the good rule and government' of an area 'in accordance with the customs and practices of the Aborigines concerned'. Aboriginal courts are enabled to exercise their jurisdiction 'having regard to the usages and customs of the community within its area' except for infringements of the regulations.

The regulations, which were not available at the time of writing this report, are enabled to make provision for 'the development, assimilation and integration of Aborigines'. The Pocket Oxford Dictionary defines 'to assimilate' as 'to make or become like, absorb, be absorbed into the system'. Such regulations could be aimed at making Aborigines like Europeans and absorbing them into the mainstream of Queensland society in such a way that their unique culture would be lost.

News commentator, Andrew Stewart, says:

> He (the Minister for Aboriginal and Island Affairs) denies the Government is putting pressure on the communities to allow tourism, mining and other developments so they will become self-sufficient at the cost of their cultures.

> The Government holds one point to push the communities into its ethos of self-sufficiency government funding. Although some reserves will reach self-sufficiency, they will still depend like any local authority on government grants.

> 'Since we'll be providing most of the funding to the communities for some time to come we have the right

not to fund them', said Mr Katter. 'But it would be extraordinary if we had to use that right ...'[94]

The *Sunday Mail* reported that 'Aboriginals dancing, working cattle, starring in rodeos, and painting each other's bodies will become major Queensland tourist attractions under plans proposed by the Aboriginals and Islanders Advancement Minister, Mr Katter'.[95]

The Yarrabah Council is not opposed to tourism as long as it is community controlled so as to minimise its cultural threat and ensure that the financial benefits remain within the community. However, as mentioned earlier, they are very opposed to the concept of public roads which will allow tourists to drive in, 'gawk' at the community and contribute nothing to it.

Under the Community Services (Aborigines) Act, people can move onto Yarrabah for lawful purposes at the invitation of community members, and could then form liaisons with Aborigines, share land, help finance them in business activities, perhaps become an economic force within the community and, if the regulations permit, vote for and stand for election to the Aboriginal council.

In fact, it is unclear from the Community Services (Aborigines) Act whether such Europeans or Asians can legally be considered 'Aborigines'. Section 6 defines 'Aborigine' as 'a person who is a descendent of an indigenous inhabitant of Australia other than the Torres Strait Islands and includes any person who resides in an area as part of a community of Islanders'. (The word 'Islanders' is no doubt a printing error for 'Aborigines'.) Section 66 says, '(1) Subject to this Part - (a) an Aborigine or other person who, in either case, is a member of the community resident in an area; ... is authorised to enter upon, be in and reside in that area'.

---

[94] *The Cairns Post*, 24 April 1984, pp. 4,6.
[95] *Sunday Mail*, 15 April 1984.

Certainly a great deal of cultural and social stress will be placed on Yarrabah Aborigines by the Community Services (Aborigines) Act. Tribal and customary marriages are no longer recognised by the Queensland Government, because no mention is made of them in the Community Services (Aborigines) Act. This will affect more isolated traditional communities to a greater extent than Yarrabah. Special provisions for recognising tribal and customary law principles in relation to the administration of the estates of intestate Aborigines have been repealed and should be restored in a form acceptable to the Aboriginal community.

5. Equality before the law

(a) Equal court treatment

'The right to equal treatment before the tribunals and all other organs administering justice' is set down in Article 5(a) of the Convention. Section 44 of the Community Services (Aborigines) Act provides that residents, whether Aborigines or not, come under the jurisdiction of the Aboriginal court. On the other hand, 'a person, whether an Aborigine or not, who is a resident in an area by reason only that he holds an appointment that requires his residence there shall not be taken to be part of the community that resides in the area' (s.44(2)) and so is subject to the magistrates court not the Aboriginal court.

Although most residents will be Aborigines and most appointees will be Europeans, this does not distinguish on the basis of race but on the basis of whether a person is a resident or an appointee. It is discriminatory that residents cannot elect to have their cases heard in a magistrates court if they so wish.

No provision was made for special Aboriginal courts under the Local Government (Aboriginal Lands) Act 1978. The courts held at Aurukun and Mornington Island are regular magistrates courts constituted by two Aboriginal justices of the peace. The rights of residents on trust areas would be increased if this lead was followed, along with training for Aboriginal justices.

'The jurisdiction of the Aboriginal Court is unlimited as regards the amount of any civil claim (should be Small Claims Court jurisdiction) and has no appeal provision for civil disputes.'[96] This may be an oversight in the Community Services (Aborigines) Act which will be amended. However, it has the effect of disadvantaging residents before the law.

An improvement in the Community Services (Aborigines) Act is that s.45 enables persons convicted in an Aboriginal court to have the 'same right of appeal against or review of the conviction and order' as if it were a magistrates court.

(b) Legal representation

The Community Services (Aborigines) Act is silent about legal representation in the Aboriginal courts, although Article 14.3(b) of the Covenant sets down the right in full equality for a person 'to have adequate time and facilities for the preparation of his defence and to communicate with counsel of his own choosing'.

(c) Justices of the Peace

In order to give residents equality before the law, s.42(2)(b) of the Community Services (Aborigines) Act enabling Aboriginal councillors to sit as members of an Aboriginal court should be repealed. It is a principle of jurisprudence that those who make the laws (council by-laws) should not sit in judgment over them.

The appointment of Aboriginal justices is not discussed in the Community Services (Aborigines) Act. At the NAC Palm Island workshops attended by Yarrabah councillors, consensus was that the 'appointment of the JPs to the Court to be the same procedure as

---

[96] National Aboriginal Council Palm Island Workshop 8–11 May 1984, Report, p.19. Unpublished, held by Queensland NAC.

normal court systems, but that there be consultation with community through the Council'.[97]

(d) The Liquor Act

To achieve the equality before the law guaranteed by the Racial Discrimination Act, the Liquor Act should apply on Queensland Aboriginal communities consonant with the principles of self-determination. The inequalities likely to be imposed by the Community Services (Aborigines) Act and Regulations are discussed in part D.6. 'Canteen and Alcohol'.

(e) Orwellian scrutiny

Sections 11 and 12 of the Community Services (Aborigines) Act 1984 provide for an Orwellian-type scrutiny of Aboriginal communities, hardly providing them with equality before the law guaranteed by the Racial Discrimination Act. Visiting justices will visit Yarrabah and other communities once every three months and under s.11(d) are requested to 'report to the Under-Secretary as soon as is practicable after completion of their visit on –

> (i) administration of the area;
> (ii) matters that in their opinion affect the welfare of residents in the area; and
> (iii) such other matters as the Under-Secretary requests.'

This visiting justice system is usually known only in prisons!

Under s.12(i), 'The Governor-in-Council may authorise any person to make and hold such inspections, investigations and inquiries for the purposes of this Act as he considers desirable'. The Queensland Government already has the power to set up commissions of inquiry so the inclusion of this power in the Community Services

---

[97] ibid. Appendix p.6.

(Aborigines) Act hardly seems necessary, unless the key is that 'any person' may be so authorised.

VI.
YARRABAH AND LAND RIGHTS

A. Relationship of land rights and self-management

To achieve political and economic self-determination, Yarrabah people need an economic base from which to work—the land and its resources. For personal liberation and cultural pride, they need to be able to turn to the land and its dreaming.

The chairman of Yarrabah put it aptly when he asked this question: 'If we haven't got land rights, what've we got to manage anyway?'

B. Land Act (Aboriginal and Islander Land Grants) Amendment Act 1982 (Qld)

I. What is it?

The Community Services (Aborigines) Act is designed as complementary management legislation to the Deed of Grant in Trust legislation (the Land Act (Aboriginal and Islander Land Grants) Amendment Act 1982: DOGIT), which is the land legislation applicable to Queensland reserves.

A matter of concern is that the Community Services (Aborigines) Act is not dependent on the Deed of Grant in Trust legislation. Section 6 of the Community Services (Aborigines) Act defines 'trust area' as 'land granted in trust by the Governor in Council for the benefit of Aboriginal inhabitants or reserved and set apart by the Governor in Council for the benefit of Aborigines under the provisions of law relating to Crown lands'.

DOGIT was not enacted until early May 1984, and at the time of writing no deeds have been granted or made available for public perusal. There have been no formal consultations with Aborigines as to the actual land covered by such deeds. There is a possibility that there will still be a considerable time lapse before the grant.

In introducing amendments to DOGIT, the Minister for Aboriginal and Island Affairs said, in December 1983:

> The Bill is designed to further secure the legal tenure of the Aboriginal and Islander people who will hold in trust under a deed of grant those areas presently reserved for Aboriginal and Islander residents' rights of occupation and land management for themselves and their children that are complete and beyond interference except by a special Act of Parliament.

> The proposals of which this Bill is part are superior to any other, because they give a perpetual title that is absolutely inalienable unless the Parliament, for some reason, decides otherwise by a special Act. Only the Parliament can alter the size of the area covered by the deed or take the deed away from the Aboriginal or Islander trustees.[98]

2. Yarrabah s response

(a) Council

(i) Amendments requested 26 January 1984

---

[98] Queensland, Legislative Assembly, *Hansard*, 1983, vol.292, p.866.

In response to the minister's speech, the chairman of Yarrabah Council, Cr Roy Gray, sent the following letter to the minister on 26 January:

Ref: The Minister's Second Reading Speech on 16/12/83 relating to the Land Act (Aboriginal and Island Land Grant) Amendment Bill.

This Council believes that the *Deed of Grant in Trust* under the Land Act 1962 as amended to date as presently offered to Aborigines by the State of Queensland, requires a number of modifications before we could be satisfied with it. It is our opinion that:-

The requirement that the Minister approve all leases for occupancy of land the subject of a Deed of Grant (Section 343, 345 and 350) is not acceptable. The Trustee should have an unrestricted right to lease or permit occupation to Aboriginal people, groups and corporations or permit them to occupy or use land.

The Trustee need not have any right to lease to non-Aboriginal persons but merely a right to allow *occupancy* or use or to issue occupancy licenses. Section 348 is a sufficient safeguard to use against action of the Trustees which is contrary to the public interest.

There should be no exclusions from the areas of land presently reserved when the Deeds are granted (Section 344C). The Trustees should hold the land presently used by Government Departments, and all buildings presently used by Aboriginal people or for enterprises in which they are employed. Government Departments should be allowed the right to occupy buildings necessary for their proposed functions, which rights would be granted by the Trustee.

Reservations from the grants for public purposes (ss.344D) should not occur. Where it appears necessary to create a public work, it will generally be in the interests of the Trustees, and the people they represent, so that such works will be able to be conducted with their consent. Any work not of that kind ought to be subject to the usual conditions of compulsory acquisition, with compensation.

The Government ought not to have the power to remove Trustees (s.340). Trustees ought to be subject only to the power of their electors to remove them by petition. Furthermore, it will be necessary that Trustees continue to hold office as title holders (with limited powers to deal with the land) during the period from their dismissal until they are replaced at a fresh election. It would be unacceptable for the title at any time to vest in a non-Aboriginal Administrator.

The Council cannot be satisfied about the quality of the title they will receive until they are aware of their rights to participate in and control mining, fishing, forestry, quarrying and the conduct of enterprises in general within the community. The Council believes that it should have full control and power to regulate what occurs upon and under the land and, to a three-mile limit from the Coast, upon the sea adjacent to its land.[99]

(ii) Land claimed 29 February 1984

On 29 February 1984, in a letter to the Minister for Aboriginal and Islander Affairs, the Yarrabah Council put in a land claim for the community. It includes former reserve land excised for defence purposes (False Cape) and for a lighthouse (Rocky Island), neither of which piece of land is still used for the purpose for which it was taken. Also part of the claim is land, traditionally considered part of the community, now used for tourist purposes (Green Island and Fitzroy Island). Little Fitzroy Island is used only by the community. Lands excised from the reserve for hospital, school, DAIA (DCS) and official purposes are also included, as are water rights. It may be that the Queensland Government will not be willing to grant a deed that recovers land already excised, even though some of it is unused except by the Yarrabah community. Water rights are not included in the Queensland legislation.

The letter read as follows:

> We anticipate that in the not too distant future it is intended to grant to this Council by way of Deed in Trust lands at Yarrabah.

> We wish to point out to you the areas of land which should be the subject of this deed. They comprise the land shown green on plan NA 352-001(B1) annexed hereto being:

---

[99] Letter from Cr Roy Gray, Chairman of Yarrabah Council to Mr. Bob Katter, Minister for Aboriginal and Island Affairs, 26 January 1984, p.l. Unpublished, held by Yarrabah Council.

(1) The Reserve for the Benefit of Aboriginal Inhabitants of the State of about 154.4 sq.km. (formerly R.204).

(2) Rocky Island being 12.14 ha (formerly R340 Reserve for Aboriginals).

(3) Lot 146 (formerly SL 28467) of 4047 sq.m.

(4) Lot 147 Res. 1171 reserved for hospital purposes being 2529 sq.m.

(5) Lot 149 being 2141 sq.m.

(6) Lot 151 being 8840 sq.m.

(7) Lot formerly SL42003 being 779 sq.m.

(8) Lot 162 R.1275 School Reserve 1.333 ha.

(9) Lot 165 R.1270(Pt.) Departmental and Official purposes reserve being 3.465 ha.

(10) Lot 166 R.1296(Pt.) being 2276 sq.m.

(11) False Cape together with the whole of the land comprised in Fitzroy Island and Green Island and Little Fitzroy Island.

In respect to all land abovementioned we also claim that we should hold title and control over the land from the high water to the low water mark and the seas and seabed from the low water mark to three (3) miles therefrom in relation to all areas of land adjacent to the sea together with Sudbury Reef, Scott Reef and Fitzroy Sandbank. (Appendix A.)[100]

(iii) Cairns workshop 29–30 March 1981

At a workshop by the writer entitled 'Aspirations of Cairns Aborigines Re Local and Self-Management and Human Rights' held at

---

[100] Letter from Cr Roy Gray, Chairman of Yarrabah Council to Mr. Bob Katter, Minister for Aboriginal and Island Affairs on 29 February 1984 p.1. Unpublished, held by Yarrabah Council.

Kuiyam Hostel, Cairns on 29–30 March, the conference voted unanimously in favour of a motion moved by the deputy chairman of Yarrabah, Cr Mick Connolly:[101]

> That this Conference welcomes the Queensland Government's legislation to give some form of land tenure to Queensland Aboriginal reserves but we believe the following five points brought up by the Yarrabah Council should be made into amendments to the Deed of Grant in Trust legislation so that adequate security of tenure and self-management can be achieved. Also that the Human Rights Commission take this matter up with the Queensland Government. (The five points are those outlined in the Council's letter of 26 January to the Minister.)

The chairman and deputy chairman of Yarrabah voted on the following motion, which was carried unanimously:

> That the Human Rights Commission request the Queensland Government to provide maps of the proposed Deed of Grant areas to Aboriginal Councils so that they have adequate time to determine whether areas granted are in line with what the Aboriginal communities have historically believed to be their boundaries. It is also recommended that surveying be done by the Australian Survey Office in consultation with Aboriginal Councils and elders on reserve/deed boundaries.

---

[101] Conference on Aspirations of Cairns Aborigines re Local- and Self-Management and Human Rights, Cairns, 29–30 March 1984, *Resolutions*, p.3. See Appendix C.

(b) Public response

(i) Public meeting 8 April 1984

The land matters brought up by the Yarrabah community at a public meeting with the minister on 8 April were the following:[102]

- fear by residents who lived outside the village area, e.g. Back Beach and Buddabadoo that they would be moved back into the village and lose their land;
- worry that King Beach, which is of particular significance to the Gunggandji tribe, might be excised from the reserve for public purposes, e.g. a tourist complex, and worry that a public access road would be built to King Beach;
- annoyance at excisions for government departments. It was felt to be segregation for land to be excised from the reserve for staff housing. This land should be leased from the council. 'Otherwise the whiteman can smoke marijuana and run inside his house and poke his tongue at us. It's called the Deed of Grant in Trust and it's about time the trust came from the government to us', said Cr Mick Connolly, deputy chairman, backing up points expressed by the community;
- concern that DOGIT does not provide mining and quarrying rights and fishing rights to the five-mile limit;
- desire for compensation for land excised from the reserve;
- desire for inalienable freehold title instead of deed of grant in trust title;
- worry about the ability of the government to excise land for public purposes (s.334D of the Land Act says 'there may be reserved from the grant a specified area, with or without describing so as to identify it the part or parts of the land

---

[102] Public Meeting Yarrabah, 8 April 1984. Author's unpublished record.

comprising that area for public purposes, with or without specifying the particular purposes.');
- the public supported the council's five requested amendments to DOGIT;
- the share farmers were 'scared stiff' that they might have their land taken from them.

Briefly, the minister's position was:

- that the council would probably be trustees and could grant title deeds to those living outside the village but there were 82 MPs who could change this;
- the government could come along anytime and resume land, e.g. for a freeway. The government could just pass another set of laws. The security of Aborigines was as great as anyone else's in Queensland;
- if the government appointed the council as trustee, it would own the houses. Maybe people could buy houses from the council. The council would receive rent, rates or house repayments. Whoever owns the land owns the houses;
- freehold means people can sell land and Aborigines had told him they did not want to be able to sell it;
- the Teachers' Union and the Police Union had asked for the right to privacy in their homes and offices. They issued an ultimatum to the government that they would pull out otherwise;
- the 'drunken riot' at Edward River played up by the media gave some government members the general feeling Aborigines are not ready. They think Yarrabah will 'go up in smoke in minutes and people will be locked up'. He was not 'Mr Popularity' in the 'outside world' because of this.

After the minister left the meeting, there was a heated argument between some residents and the manager over timber rights and particularly access by Aborigines to red cedar to make their own furniture, when the white staff seemed to have access to it. Privileged access by Europeans to the sawmill after hours was brought up as well as the suspected removal from the reserve of red cedar for sale. The manager said Aborigines could apply to him for red cedar, which was in short supply, and it was being used where it could best be used, which was for office furniture. The council requested that timber rights be given to it.

(ii) Public meeting 18 May 1984

At the public meeting called to discuss the beer canteen, Mr Colin Neal of the Yarrabah Co-operative said, 'We don't want to discuss the pub. We want to discuss the land issue. We can't control anything without the land'.

C. What are land rights

1. Holding goals

Following consultation with Aborigines, the Federal Minister for Aboriginal Affairs Mr Clyde Holding, set down the following goals for any land rights legislation which he considered fundamental.[103]

(1) Aboriginal land to be held under inalienable freehold title.
(2) Protection of sacred sites.
(3) Aboriginal control of mining on Aboriginal land.
(4) Access to mining royalty equivalents.
(5) Compensation for loss of land to be negotiated.

---

[103] Greg McIntyre, Do the Deeds of Grant in Trust and Community Services (Aborigines) Act achieve the fundamental goals of land rights? 23 April 1984 p.1. Unpublished, held by Greg McIntyre.

2. Brennan requisites

Barrister and Catholic priest, Frank Brennan SJ, who has followed the legislation carefully at the request of the Catholic Bishops, identifies five legal requirements for land rights/inalienable freehold.[104] Numbers one and three simply add up to inalienable freehold. The others are an addition to Mr Holding's principles:

> 2. Integrity of reserve boundaries.
>
> 4. Ancillary rights (including timber, quarry, hunting, foraging and mineral).
>
> 5. Trustees control of land free from bureaucratic constraints and political interference by government.

3. Baume principles

Under the Fraser government, Senator Peter Baume established similar principles when he was Minister for Aboriginal Affairs: security of tenure, integrity of present reserve boundaries and self-management. He also laid down a fourth principle:

> (4) Full consultation with Aborigines and Torres Strait Islanders before any decision is made.[105]

4. North Queensland Land Council objectives

Pre-dating all these, the North Queensland Land Council, in consultation with delegates from all Aboriginal reserves in North

---

[104] Frank Brennan S.J., A comparison of Deeds of Grant in Trust (Amended) with Aboriginal Land Rights (N.T.) Act 1976. Consultation document No.6, 19 December 1983, p.4. Unpublished held by Qld Catholic Bishops.
[105] Greg McIntyre, op.cit.

Queensland as far south as Yarrabah and Palm Island, established the following policy at its inaugural meeting in January 1976.[106]

> 1. Immediate ownership of tribal land by respective tribal groups.
>
> 2. That all Aboriginal Reserves be handed over to the respective Aboriginal groups, and that the land be effectively controlled and owned by the Aborigines in that area under their law and customs.
>
> 3. That Aboriginal lands include total rights to all natural resources, and that present mining and prospecting be suspended until negotiations are held with Aborigines.
>
> 4. That land ownership and control be legally protected and regarded as inviolable.
>
> 5. That Aboriginal people be compensated for the loss of all Aboriginal-designated reserves, tribal lands, and other lands revoked by the Commonwealth and state governments.
>
> 6. That before compensation is decided, negotiations be held to acquire those lands plus any other lands deemed necessary by the respective Aboriginal groups and tribal groups for their survival and benefit.
>
> 7. That any 'Crown land' which is of traditional or sacred significance to Aborigines be granted without fees or constraints.

---

[106] North Queensland Land Council Inaugural Meeting, Cairns, *Minutes*, January 1976. Cited in *N.Q. Messagestick*, January 1976.

D. Comparison of Land Act (Aboriginal & Islander Land Grants) Amendment Act 1982 (Qld) with land rights

1. Inalienable freehold

This is the only land rights principle to which DOGIT addresses itself. Even then, there are a few problems. Solicitor for the Yarrabah Council, Mr Greg McIntyre, writes:

> The Deed of Grant in Trust under Section 334 of the Land Act of 1962 is not a 'Deed of Grant in Fee Simple' (or Freehold) in accordance with Forms 1, 1A or 1B of the Act, it is a 'Grant ... upon Trust for the Benefit of Aboriginal and Islander inhabitants', in accordance with Form 2. It is different from Freehold in that it may revert to the Crown if the Trusts, Conditions, Reservations and Provisos of the Act, and in the Deed (relating to Crown ownership of Gold, Minerals and Petroleum) are not complied with.

> The title is inalienable insofar as it can be surrendered to the Crown or transferred to another Local Authority or corporate body with the approval of the Governor in Council. Otherwise it cannot be sold or transferred (s.342 Land Act). The title may further be alienated by way of Mortgage with the consent of the Governor in Council (s.351 Land Act).[107]

Although the 1983 Amendments to DOGIT ensure that an Act of Parliament is required to revoke all or part of the deed of grant, the Governor-in-Council is enabled on the making of the grant to reserve from the grant 'a specified area, with or without describing so as to

---

[107] Greg McIntyre, op. cit., p.1–2.
The Aboriginal Land Rights (N.T.) Act 1976 does not allow such alienation by mortgage default.

identify it the part or parts of the land comprising that area, for public purposes, with or without specifying the particular purpose or purposes' (s.334D). This is a big worry to Yarrabah residents. Cr Mick Connolly has dubbed it the 'hovering clause', ready to pounce like a vulture on Aboriginal land.

Frank Brennan in his Consultation Document No. 6 recommended top-up Commonwealth legislation:

> If the Commonwealth Parliament were to make a law providing for the automatic transfer of any Aboriginal land resumed by a State Government to an Aboriginal trust, then Aboriginal communities would be assured the most secure form of tenure possible. ... If the Commonwealth Parliament in turn revoked Aboriginal title to land, any Aboriginal community so affected would have the constitutional guarantee of receiving just compensation.[108]

2. Protection of sacred sites

The Community Services (Aborigines) Act and DOGIT make no mention of sacred sites. The only Act in Queensland which refers to sacred sites is the Aboriginal Relics Preservation Act which is administered by DAIA's archaeology branch and applies only to man-modified objects or sites. Sacred sites become the property of the state and can only be declared on private property if the owner agrees, in which case traditional use is allowed.

Yarrabah Council requested of the minister on 19 March that Aboriginal Advisory Council (now Aboriginal Co-ordinating Council) representatives be members of an Archaeology Branch Board which they expected to be set up under the Community Services (Aborigines)

---

[108] Frank Brennan SJ, op. cit., p.5–6.

Act to ensure some Aboriginal participation in decision-making.[109] Such a board was not set up and the Aboriginal Co-ordinating Council has been given no role in relation to sacred sites. Aborigines are not happy that sacred sites in Queensland are the property of the state and that only man-modified objects and sites are able to be declared.

The federal minister, Mr Clyde Holding, has had interim national heritage legislation passed by the federal parliament to protect sites of significance which may be under threat.

3. Mining—Aboriginal control and royalties

The Queensland Aborigines Act 1971 allowed the trustee of reserves (the director of DAIA) to negotiate a mining agreement, including participation in the profits of the mining venture, before allowing exploration or mining on reserves. All mention of mining has been omitted from the Community Services (Aborigines) Act so that Aborigines living on Queensland reserves or trust areas have fewer mineral rights than before—in fact none. No more royalties will be paid. Section 22(2) of DOGIT says 'the Governor in Council shall have regard to the views of and any recommendations made by the trustee'. That is, Aboriginal councils can give advice but have no veto powers under DOGIT. In this respect, there is little change from previous legislation.

Frank Brennan comments that:

> The Mining Act contains detailed provisions for compensation to occupiers of Crown Land and of private land. Similar provisions do not exist for occupiers of lands the subject of deeds of grant in trust. (See Mining Act Pt.IV, Division IV and Pt. XIII of s.44(4)). A Council will be powerless

---

[109] Yarrabah Council Meeting, Yarrabah, 19 March 1984 P.3. Unpublished, held by Yarrabah Council.

to take out its own authorities to prospect unless the Governor in Council gives approval.[110]

The Yarrabah Council is making moves at the moment to take out its own authority to prospect over the whole reserve/trust area. The Yarrabah community and council have said many times that they want mineral rights. Such rights would have to include veto 'power, provision for payment of mining royalty equivalents, and authorities to prospect and mine themselves if they so wished'.

The North Queensland Land Council maintains that present mining and prospecting in Queensland should be suspended until negotiations are held with Aborigines in an effort to remedy past injustices. There is substantial support for the North Queensland Land Council at Yarrabah.

Mr Neville Harper, Member for Auburn (NP) a member of parliament, asked the Minister for Mines and Energy a Question Upon Notice on 24 March 1982 on whether mineral rights attached to any lands other than Crown lands in Queensland. The answer was:

> (1) ... Coal on or below the surface of land that was alienated in fee simple by the Crown before 1 March 1910 is the property of the owner of that land for royalty purposes (with a few exceptions). Other than gold and coal, the rights to certain other minerals attach to land alienated pursuant to the Crown Lands Alienation Act of 1868 and the Mineral Lands Act of 1872. Titles to such lands are generally referred to as mineral freeholds or mineral selections. ...

---

[110] Frank Brennan S.J. *Consultation documents on services legislation for Aborigines and Torres Strait Islanders in Queensland*, 10 December 1982, p.82. Booklet produced by Qld Catholic Bishops, Brisbane. See also The Land Act (Aboriginal and Islander Land Grants) Amendment Bill 1982, (Q1d) s.22 (1).

Coal has been won in recent years from lands described in (1) situated in the Ipswich, Darling Downs and Maryborough areas. The owners of such lands have benefited by way of the payment of royalty on the coal won.

A lease to mine coal, whether the property of the Crown or not, may only be granted by the Crown. In the case of other minerals which are not the property of the Crown, it is competent for the owner of the land to which the mineral rights attach to grant a lease or to enter into any agreement or arrangement for the purpose of mining those minerals [111]

Aborigines under DOGIT have significantly fewer rights to minerals than other Queensland landholders.

4. Compensation for loss of land

There is no mention of compensation in the Deed of Grant legislation for any land resumed by an Act of the Queensland Parliament. It 'shall revert to the Crown freed and discharged from all encumbrances, estates, or interests whatsoever and may be dealt with by the Crown as if it had never been granted'.[112]

The North Queensland Land Council would like to see negotiations held to acquire any lost Aboriginal reserves, tribal and other lands before compensation is paid out.

5. Integrity of reserve boundaries

DOGIT does not describe the boundaries of the land to be granted to Queensland reserve inhabitants. In the Northern Territory legislation, the boundaries were set out in a schedule to the Act. Yarrabah is anxiously awaiting the drawing up of the deeds to see if

---

[111] Frank Brennan, S.J. Consultation document No.8. Appendix p.15. Unpublished, held by Qld Catholic Bishops Brisbane.
[112] Land Act 1962-1983 (Qld), s.353.

areas which were once part of the reserve and traditionally a part of the Yarrabah community's land—False Cape, Green Island, Fitzroy Island and Little Fitzroy Island—are included. Other reserves have similar worries, e.g. will land excised from Weipa for Comalco and not now used be returned, and will all the Palm Island group be included in the deed? What about timber reserves and cattle properties used by Aboriginal reserves?

The previous Minister for Aboriginal and Islander Advancement, Mr Tomkins, told parliament on 23 November 1982 that 'it is confirmed that the deeds of grant in trust will be based principally upon the existing Aboriginal reserve communities'. He admitted certain discrepancies in land areas, however.[113]

6. Ancillary rights

Section 17 of DOGIT amends s.45 of the Forestry Act 1959–71 so that forest and quarry products are the property of the Crown. Yarrabah Aborigines will have to apply and pay for permits. If they are not granted, it will be an offence to gather or dig forest or quarry products. This is despite the fact that these rights were given to Aurukun and Mornington Island Aborigines in s.31(2) of the Local Government (Aboriginal Lands) Act 1978.

In Brennan's analysis of DOGIT, he points out that Aborigines have less rights than most Europeans who hold pastoral tenures. '96.5% of the 146 million hectares, subject to tenures current in the books of the Lands Department as at 30 June 1980, was held as selections or pastoral tenures. Those holdings totalled 19,602 of which 88.3% were holdings giving full quarry rights ab initio, forestry rights

---

[113] Queensland, Legislative Assembly, *Hansard* 1982, vol.289, p.2535.

after two years, and being capable of conversion to freehold or perpetual lease.'[114]

Traditional hunting, foraging and fishing rights have not been guaranteed under DOGIT. The Community Services (Aborigines) Act (s.77(1) & (2)) only allows residents to hunt and fish using traditional means for their own consumption. They may not sell such products. This means they will not be able to keep commercial fishermen out of their coastal waters.

7. Freedom from bureaucratic control and political interference

a. The Community Services (Aborigines) Act 1984 (Qld)

The whole question of self-determination and self-management has been discussed in the sections dealing with the Community Services (Aborigines) Act, which is the complementary legislation to DOGIT. They reveal an amazing amount of bureaucratic control, ministerial discretion and dependence on the goodwill of the Governor-in-Council rather than on the provisions of law.

b. Leases

The trustees of land granted under DOGIT are expected to be the Aboriginal councils. This is what the minister has led the Yarrabah Council to believe but this is not spelt out in DOGIT. The trustees are not empowered to lease land without the prior approval of the minister. In fact, they cannot even sub-let, mortgage or transfer a lease without ministerial approval.[115] If a lease is approved, it may only run for seventy-five years and may not be renewed. The minister can determine whether or not the rent shall be the highest annual rent which can reasonably be charged.[116]

---

[114] Frank Brennan, S.J. *Consultation documents on services legislation for Aborigines and Torres Strait Islanders in Queensland*, 10 December 1982, p.82. Booklet produced by Qld Catholic Bishops, Brisbane.
[115] Land Act 1962-1983 (Qld), s.347.
[116] ibid., s.344.

If he/she considers it to be in the public interest, the minister may cancel a lease and any improvements by a tenant become the property of the trustees.[117] On the other hand, if the trustees cancel a lease, the minister may rescind the cancellation on receipt of an application from the lessee within twenty-one days of receiving notice of such a termination by the trustees.[118]

c. Removal of trustees

The government may remove one or all of the trustees if it is considered in the public interest to do so.[119] At least the conditions under which this can happen should be spelt out in law so that there is some protection for the trustees from intimidation.

d. Camping

Many Yarrabah Aborigines live and/or camp out in makeshift shelters and will be affected by s.350 of the Lands Act which says that persons not occupying a building may not stay on land for more than a month without the consent of the minister. They can be charged with trespassing and removed from the land by the police.[120]

e. Other

As already outlined, the government must approve mining and mortgages and permits are needed to gather timber, e.g. firewood. By-laws made by trustees are subject to the veto of the minister. Also, trustees are obliged to furnish to the minister all financial information he may require.[121] Rights are significantly less than under land rights legislation in the Northern Territory and South Australia.

8. Consultation

---

[117] ibid., s.348.
[118] ibid., s.347.
[119] ibid., s.340 (3).
[120] ibid., s.373.
[121] ibid., s.341

There has been very little consultation with Queensland Aborigines over DOGIT and the Community Services (Aborigines) Act. The Aboriginal Advisory Council meeting at Bamaga in August 1982 rejected DOGIT while alternatives were explored. A working party was set up to provide more effective consultation. When the working party tried to have a meeting, the state government would not recognise or fund it. At the end of August 1982, the working party held a meeting with the help of the Catholic Church. The state government called one meeting after that, at which the membership of the working party, including the chairmanship, was altered by departmental intervention.

9. Crown land

Point 7 of the North Queensland Land Council principles is that any 'Crown land' which is of traditional or sacred significance to Aborigines be granted 'without fees or constraints'.[122] DOGIT deals only with reserve land. There is no mechanism in Queensland for the return of Crown lands or the hearing of land claims. This is despite the fact that two-thirds of Queensland's Aboriginal population live outside the reserves.

10. Country reserves

The Commonwealth Department of Aboriginal Affairs, Cairns, estimates that there are 148.844 ha of country reserve land settled on by sixteen communities in its Cairns regional administrative area.[123] Country reserves do not have a DAIA administrative presence.

---

[122] North Queensland Land Council Inaugural Meeting, Cairns, January 1976, Minutes, cited in *N.Q. Messagestick* January 1976.
[123] Australia, Department of Aboriginal Affairs, Commonwealth paper tabled at QEF Area Advisory Committee Meeting, Cairns Country Reserves—DOGIT, February 1984.

At the Aboriginal and Islander Catholic Council Conference in Cairns in January 1984, Mr Katter said that no firm decision had been made on the future of country reserves (which are legally Crown land reserved for the benefit of Aborigines) but he was willing to consider individual applications for them to come under DOGIT.[124] Unfortunately, this would mean coming under much greater bureaucratic control because these communities could not come under DOGIT without coming under the complementary Community Services (Aborigines) Act.

Yarrabah councillors spoke in support of and voted for the following motion at a conference the writer organised in Cairns on 29–30 March 1984:

> That this meeting calls upon the Queensland Minister for Aboriginal and Islander Affairs—Bob Katter—to include all country reserves and islands that are linked traditionally and spiritually to Aboriginal people in the Deed of Grant in Trust.[125]

11. Excision—towards assimilation

Rather than deal with the topic of excisions from deeds under the heading of integrity of reserve boundaries, alienability or self-management, I am dealing with it separately because I think it is very significant. I believe it is part of the government's assimilation plan eventually to make Queensland reserves no different from any other country town.

---

[124] 11th Annual State Conference of the Aboriginal and Islander Catholic Council, Cairns 9–12 January 1984, Minutes. Unpublished, held by Aboriginal and Islander Catholic Council, Cairns.
[125] Conference on Aspirations of Cairns Aborigines re Local and Self-Management and Human Rights, Cairns, 29–30 March 1984, *Resolutions*, p.2. See Appendix C.

As far back as 5 April 1978, the then Queensland Minister for Aboriginal and Islander Advancement made a ministerial statement outlining the government's policy which is seen in action today:

> The communities provide training grounds to achieve this at a rate determined by the people themselves. It is expected that each community will eventually emerge to become a conventional town in the stream of Queensland's progress; with back-up support by the industries being developed.

> We seek an end to intelligent so-called parasitism, paternalism and a subject race totally dependent upon handouts made in the name of government initiatives under the ploy of self-determination.[126]

From this report it can be seen that Yarrabah Aborigines do not believe that they have been moving towards self-management or self-determination at their own rate. The Queensland Government has in the past legally proscribed this and is still doing so. Queensland Aboriginal laws have been and still are instruments of oppression and discrimination. Depending on the phase of Queensland Government policy, Queensland laws have also been instruments of segregation and assimilation.

I contend that the excisions are part of a whittling away process to alienate Aboriginal reserve land to the point where in ten years' time or so Aboriginal councils will have no land left to be trustees of.

Section 334C of the Land Act says that improvements to the property of the Crown will be excluded from the deed of grant. This would include schools, hospitals, police stations, Department of Community Services buildings and Queensland Government staff

---

[126] Queensland, Legislative Assembly, *Hansard*, 1978, vol.274, p.155.

houses. Also excluded will be aerodromes, landing strips, ports, roads, stock routes, bridges and railways.

In addition, s.334D of the Land Act allows a specified area (size and location unnamed) to be reserved from the deed for unspecified public purposes.

On one of his trips to Yarrabah, the minister said that commercial activity would not be included in the deed. This would mean stores, timber mills, bakeries, butchers, potteries and clothing shops etc., would be excluded from the deed whether or not these existing enterprises were owned by the Department of Community Services or the AIB.

Individual Aborigines are being encouraged for the first time to start enterprises. The Minister for Aboriginal and Island Affairs has foreshadowed the possibility of the land on which individual Aboriginal businesses and farms are run being alienated from community title under a lease from the trustees to individual title, e.g. separate deeds of grant. He has also foreshadowed Aboriginal residents receiving separate deeds for their houses. The Queensland Government until recently consistently opposed Aborigines owning land by group titles. This trend could prove a threat to traditional Aboriginal concepts and practice of community ownership.

What we would then have is a 'patchwork quilt' situation where the community is divided up into DCS land, AIB land, Queensland Department of Education land, Queensland Police Department land, public areas, community land and many small deeds for individual Aboriginal land holders. The only land over which the Yarrabah Council will be able to make by-laws is community land. This will make town planning difficult for the council, which believes the whole of Yarrabah should be community land and subject to its by-laws.

What is going to be left of the reserves in ten years' time? Will they be just another part of Queensland with a few extra black faces?

This appears to be what the Queensland Government would like to see.

Yarrabah Aborigines would like equal rights, but they also want the right to be different, which is what true equality entails. The Federal Liberal/National Country Party policy of 1975 recognised this in accepting 'the principle that all Aborigines and Torres Strait Islanders should be as free as other Australians to determine their own varied futures' and recognising 'the fundamental right of Aborigines to retain their racial identity and traditional lifestyle or where desired to adopt partially or wholly a European life style'.[127] Both the Queensland and the federal governments talk about equality, but they define it differently. Aborigines agree with federal governments that equality means the right to be different; the right to equal opportunity to determine their own futures.

The irony of Queensland Government policy is that 'the DAIA is supposed to encourage Aborigines to adopt the same loyalties and aspirations as European Australians but it reminds them of their Aboriginality every day and punishes them for it' (e.g. under-payment of award wages etc.)[128]

---

[127] *Federal Liberal/National Country Party policy* of 1975. Held by Department of Aboriginal Affairs.
[128] Daniel Craig, *The social impact of the State on an Aboriginal reserve in Queensland. Australia*, Ph.D. Thesis, University of California, Berkeley, 1979, p.176.

VII.
YARRABAH, HUMAN RIGHTS
AND LAND RIGHTS

————————◊————————

I n the No.7 issue of *Human Rights*, Newsletter of the Human Rights Commission, December 1983, Commissioner Norma Ford is reported as being 'concerned that the land rights issue has become another vehicle for the propagation of racial prejudice which could prevent the issue from being considered in a rational and informed manner'.[129]

A landmark address was given by the Deputy Chairman of the Human Rights Commission Mr Peter Bailey, to the Queensland Branch of the Institute of International Affairs in November 1983. He said:

> There could be no more important advance in the area of race discrimination than for the Queensland Government to give Aboriginal people full rights to land and control over the lives of those living on that land.[130]

He continued:

---

[129] Australia, Human Rights Commission, *Human Rights Newsletter* (No. 7 December 1983), AGPS, Canberra 1983, p.10.
[130] ibid.

Although much conscientious effort is devoted in Queensland to assist the Aboriginal people, structural changes are required, and much greater attentiveness to and active implementation of the wishes of the people themselves.

He also suggested that Queensland consider legislation to outlaw discrimination.

In conclusion, as this report shows, there is a long way to go yet in Queensland before Aborigines on reserves/trust areas like Yarrabah have basic human rights. Although structural changes have occurred in the new legislation, full rights to land and self-determination have not been achieved. Aboriginal aspirations have been largely ignored. Aborigines in Queensland have fewer rights at law than other Queenslanders and are subject to an Orwellian-type scrutiny that the rest of the community would not tolerate.

Conclusion

————◊————

A momentous change occurred in 1984. The changes since then have been no less momentous. Work on the recognition of Indigenous people in the Australian Constitution and the removal of racism from it is still in progress. The Recognise Campaign was set up to gain support for change though the issue has caused much debate because claims of sovereignty and a request for a treaty have not been met. Norman Miller presented over 5,000 signatures on the 'Miller Boomerang Petition'[131] to the federal parliament from citizens around Australia, Indigenous and non-Indigenous, in support of a referendum to change the constitution. These changes were to be along the lines of the recommendations of the Expert Panel on Constitutional Recognition of Aboriginal and Torres Strait Islander Peoples. While there has been a Joint Select Committee on the Recognition of Aboriginal and Torres Strait Islander people in the constitution, consultations are still occurring with Indigenous people, leading up to a conference in Alice Springs on 27 May 2017, the 50th anniversary of the 1967 referendum.

It was planned to have the referendum on this date but the referendum has been postponed while a referendum advisory council undertakes a number of regional conferences with Indigenous people.

---

[131] Warren Entsch presents the Boomerang Petition to Parliament on behalf of Indigenous leader Norman Miller http://www.warrenentsch.com.au/Media/Speeches/tabid/74/articleType/ArticleView/articleId/996/Presenting-the-Boomerang-Petition-to-Parliament.aspx, Miller Boomerang Petition http://youtu.be/a06cqhZfOwI

Wording to be put to a referendum has still not been put forward. Some Aboriginal people are saying that Indigenous people need to be recognised on the birth certificate of Australia and others are worried it will hold back a treaty. Indigenous Land Use agreements (ILUAs) negotiated as part of native title could usefully be seen as a number of regional treaties around Australia and be pursued more vigorously. After all, there were around 600 Aboriginal nations in Australia pre European occupation, not one. This number has been greatly reduced by colonisation. However, it is possible an overall treaty could encompass a number of regional treaties or ILUAs.

What we need to do now as Australians is to face up to the truth of the history of our nation and embrace the Uluru Statement from the Heart of 26 May 2017. The Referendum Council was appointed on 7 December 2015 to advise the Prime Minister and Leader of the Opposition on the next steps towards constitutional reform. As a result, over 250 delegates met at the 2017 First Nations National Constitutional Convention at Uluru, the heart of the nation, after a six-month consultation period. The Statement calls for the establishment of a First Nations Voice enshrined in the Constitution and the setting up of a Makarrata Commission to supervise a process of agreement-making between governments and First Nations that includes truth-telling about Indigenous history.

The Statement said that in 1967 Indigenous people were counted and in 2017 they seek to be heard. Sadly, Indigenous people were left out of the founding document of Australia in 1901 – because it was largely setting out state rights as against commonwealth rights, and Indigenous people were forgotten. The Uluru Statement has not had a warm reception from government but the story is not over yet

Yarrabah is unique in Australia as it had a coronation ceremony in its Anglican church led by its own Aboriginal Bishop Arthur Malcolm in December 2011. Vincent Jabaan Shreiber is the fifth generation to hold the title after Minminiy was made king in 1899.

While Aboriginal people did not traditionally have kings, but had a group of elders, white authorities appointed kings all over Australia who were traditionally highly respected. Yarrabah is holding onto this as it recognises their sovereignty.

While discrimination is still raising its ugly head, segregation is on its last breath and the Closing the Gap campaign is desperately trying to reduce the huge disparity in socio-economic indicators between Indigenous and non-Indigenous people in Australia.

Barbara Miller

APPENDIX A

We anticipate that in the not too distant future it is intended to grant to this Council by way of Deed in Trust lands at Yarrabah.

We wish to point out to you the areas of land which should be the subject of this deed. They comprise the land shown green on plan NA 352-001(B1) annexed hereto being:

(1) The Reserve for the Benefit of Aboriginal Inhabitants of the State of about 154.4 sq.km. (formerly R.204).

(2) Rocky Island being 12.14 ha (formerly R340 Reserve for Aboriginals).

(3) Lot 146 (formerly SL 28467) of 4047 sq.m.

(4) Lot 147 Res. 1171 reserved for hospital purposes being 2529 sq.m.

(5) Lot 149 being 2141 sq.m.

(6) Lot 151 being 8840 sq.m.

(7) Lot formerly SL42003 being 779 sq.m.

(8) Lot 162 R.1275 School Reserve 1.333 ha.

(9) Lot 165 R.1270(Pt.) Departmental and Official purposes reserve being 3.465 ha.

(10) Lot 166 R.1296(Pt.) being 2276 sq.m.

(11) False Cape together with the whole of the land comprised in Fitzroy Island and Green Island and Little Fitzroy Island.

In respect to all land abovementioned we also claim that we should hold title and control over the land from the high water to the low water mark and the seas and seabed from the low water mark to three (3) miles therefrom in relation to all areas of land adjacent to the sea together with Sudbury Reef, Scott Reef and Fitzroy Sandbank.

APPENDIX B

FORM 5

ABORIGINES ACT 1971 (SECTION 24)

PERMIT TO VISIT A RESERVE

This permit authorises the person/s named herein to visit the Reserve between 29-7-1977 and 27-8-1977 unless sooner revoked.

SURNAME: Burns   CHRISTIAN NAMES: Lloyd

COUNCIL CHAIRWOMAN/DIRECTOR

DATE: 27/7/77   A.D. Yeatman

This permit shall not be granted for any period exceeding one month.

FORM 4

ABORIGINES ACT 1971 (SECTION 20)

PERMIT TO RESIDE ON A RESERVE

This permit authorises Robert Smallwood & Family, and his/her spouse and children, namely Una, subject to the conditions endorsed hereon, to reside on the Yarrabah Reserve.

Date: 9th September 1977 Council Chairman

Date:

Director

This permit shall remain in force until the 9th day of October, 1977 *unless sooner revoked.*

Conditions of Permit

1. That you satisfactorily perform duties allocated to you by the Yarrabah Council and from Police Sergeant Wilcox as a Community Policeman.

2. That through your action you demonstrate to the Council the will and ability to become an accepted member of this Community.

A.D. Yeatman

Chairlady - Yarrabah Council

APPENDIX C

ASPIRATIONS OF CAIRNS ABORIGINES

RE LOCAL AND SELF MANAGEMENT AND HUMAN RIGHTS

KUIYAM HOSTEL. CAIRNS 29-30/3/84

RESOLUTIONS

1. That the Human Rights Commission be commended for using Aboriginal and Islander Chairpersons for recent Compulsory Conferences in Cairns and this practice be continued and that monetary compensation for the injury of being discriminated against is a step in the right direction.
    MOVED: MICK CONNOLLY
    SECONDED: MARIE WALLACE

2. That the Human Rights Commission should institute a public awareness campaign on affirmative action because of the community backlash it is causing e.g. in employment programmes and Aboriginal Study and Secondary Grants Schemes.
    MOVED: EVELYN SCOTT
    SECONDED: DANNY DE BUSH

3. That the Cairns Consultative Committee on Community Relations encourage owners of public bars in Cairns to adopt more relaxed standards of dress suitable to the tropics e.g. T-shirts, thongs or bare feet should be acceptable. Aborigines from the bush are often refused service because of their dress particularly because of not wearing shoes.

MOVED: CLARRIE GROGAN
SECONDED: MERVYN AHKEE

4. That the Human Rights Commission work towards the changing of the Racial Discrimination Act 1975 so that the onus is not back on the complainant to take court action if conciliation fails. It is noted that under the Sex Discrimination Act 1983 the Sex Discrimination Commissioner can refer a matter not able to be conciliated to the Human Rights Commission which can then hold on inquiry and make a determination. The complainant or the Commission can seek an order in the Federal Court to enforce such a determination. A similar provision should be provided in the Racial Discrimination Act 1975.

MOVED: EVELYN SCOTT
SECONDED: MICK MILLER

5. That the Human Rights Commission expedite proceedings to resolve the issue of non-payment of award wages on Qld Aboriginal reserves.

MOVED: GEOFF GUEST
SECONDED: BILL HOLLINGSWORTH

6. That the Human Rights Commission expedite proceedings to resolve the issue of the refusal by the Qld Lands Department to transfer the lease of Archer River Bend to John Koowarta and the Winchanan group.

MOVED: MICK MILLER

SECONDED: MERV AHKEE

7. That the Cairns Consultative Committee on Community Relations be given more power by the Human Rights Commission to conciliate locally cases of infringements of human rights. Also that there be more feedback from the Human Rights Commission office in Canberra to the Cairns Consultative Committee e.g. notification of cases received directly by Canberra and the progress of all cases involving this area.
> MOVED: MERV AHKEE
> SECONDED: ROY GRAY

8. That the Human Rights Commission write a letter to the National press asking for Aborigines to be employed in the field of advertising on TV and in newspapers.
> MOVED: MICK CONNOLLY
> SECONDED: NANETTE AHMAT

9. That the Human Rights Commission take up with the Qld Health Department the upgrading of hospitals on Aboriginal communities in Cape York Peninsula and that qualified medical and nursing personnel be attached to these hospitals. (As it stands, all ante-natal cases have to come to Cairns for confinement.)
> MOVED: MARJ BALDWIN
> SECONDED: DALE CLAUSSEN

10. That the Human Rights Commission take up with the Qld Department of Aboriginal and Islander Advancement (DAIA) and Community Councils the supply of fresh healthy food products to the stores on Aboriginal communities in Queensland.
> MOVED: MARJ BALDWIN
> SECONDED: MERV AHKEE

11. That the Human Rights Commission take up with the DAIA and Community Councils that the standard of housing and sanitation on Aboriginal communities in Queensland be upgraded because it causes environmental health hazards.

    MOVED: MARJ BALDWIN

    SECONDED: JIM LEFTWICH

12. That the Human Rights Commission take up with the Qld Health Department the appointment of Aborigines to the local hospital boards of their area. Also that the Cairns Consultative Committee on Community relations take this matter up with the Cairns Hospital Board.

    MOVED: MARJ BALDWIN

    SECONDED: MICK CONNOLLY

13. That the Human Rights Commission take positive action to rectify the stilted perspective generated in the teaching of history in that Aboriginal prehistory is taught while omitting comparative details of European and Asiatic prehistory.

    MOVED: HUGH SKINNER

    SECONDED: GEOFF GUEST

14. That this meeting calls upon the Qld Minister for Aboriginal and Islander Affairs—Bob Katter—to include all country reserves and islands that are linked traditionally and spiritually to Aboriginal people in the Deed of Grant in Trust.

    MOVED: MICK MILLER

    SECONDED: MARJ BALDWIN

15. That this conference welcomes the Qld Government's legislation to give some form of land tenure to Qld Aboriginal reserves but we believe the following 5 points brought up by the Yarrabah Council

should be made into amendments to the Deed of Grant in Trust legislation so the adequate security of tenure and self-management can be achieved. Also that the Human Rights Commission take this matter up with the Qld government.

a) The requirement that the Minister approve all leases for occupancy of land the subject of a Deed of Grant (s.343, 345 and 350) is not acceptable. The Trustee should have an unrestricted right to lease or permit occupation to Aboriginal people groups and corporations or permit them to occupy or use land. The Trustee need not have any right to lease to non-Aboriginal persons but merely a right to allow occupancy.

b) There should be no exclusions from the areas of land presently reserved when the Deeds are granted (s.344C). The Trustees should hold the land presently used by Government Departments, and all buildings presently used by Aboriginal people or for enterprises in which they are employed. Government Departments should be allowed the right to occupy buildings necessary for their proposed functions, which rights would be granted by the Trustee.

c) Reservations from the grants for public purposes (s.344D) should not occur. Where it appears necessary to create a public work, it will generally be in the interests of the Trustees, and the people they represent so that such works will be able to be conducted with their consent. Any work not of that kind ought to be subject to the usual conditions of compulsory acquisition, with compensation.

d) The Government ought not to have the power to remove Trustees (s.340). Trustees ought to be subject only to the power of their electors to remove them by petition. Furthermore, it will be necessary that Trustees continue to hold office as title holders (with limited powers to deal with the land) during the period from their dismissal until they are replaced at a fresh election. It would be unacceptable for the title at any time to vest in a non-aboriginal Administrator.

e) The Council cannot be satisfied about the quality of the title they will receive until they are aware of their rights to participate in and control mining, fishing, forestry, quarrying and the, conduct of enterprises in general within their community. The Council believes that it should have full control and power to regulate what occurs upon and under the land and, to a three-mile limit from the Coast, upon the sea adjacent to its land.

MOVED: MICK CONNOLLY
SECONDED: NANETTE AHMAT

16. That the Human Rights Commission request that a draft copy of the new Services Legislation be circulated widely by the Qld Government for discussion amongst the Qld community and that adequate consultation time be given to Aborigines on Qld reserves.
MOVED: JOE McGUINESS
SECONDED: ROY GRAY

17. That the Human Rights Commission request the Qld Government to provide maps of the proposed Deed of Grant areas to Aboriginal Councils so that they have adequate time to determine whether areas granted are in line with what the Aboriginal Communities have historically believed to be their boundaries. It is also recommended

that surveying be done by the Australian Survey Office in consultation with Aboriginal Councils and elders on reserve/deed boundaries.
    MOVED: MARIE WALLACE
    SECONDED: SYD GRAY

18. That the Human Rights Commission take up with the Qld Government the need to transfer the DAIA housing function in urban communities to local Aboriginal Housing Societies.
    MOVED: DANNY DE BUSH
    SECONDED: JIM LEFTWICH

APPENDIX D
1984 RECOMMENDATIONS

1. That the Human Rights Commission be notified that one month is insufficient time to consult adequately with Aborigines of Cairns and Yarrabah on our aspirations on local management and human rights and write a document.

2. That another meeting be convened of all Aboriginal and Islander Welfare organisations in Cairns to form an Aboriginal Welfare Council to:

   a) be responsible for the distribution of Emergency Relief Funds and

   b) rationalize the delivery of welfare services.

3. That in future the Aboriginal Training and Cultural Institute be utilized and supported as too many Non-Aboriginals are being used to train our people.

APPENDIX E

━━━━◄━━━━

Table 1: Human Rights Issues Raised by the Queensland By-Laws

By Law		Racial Discrimination Convention	Wide Discretion
All by-laws	Art.25 26	Art.5(c)	
Ch.4 by-law 1(g)	19		
Ch.4 by-law 1(h)	19,21,22		
Ch.5 by-law 1	7,17,26	Art.5	
Ch.6		Art.5	
Ch.8 by-laws 5,6	17		Yes
Ch.10 by-law 1	17,19		Yes
Ch.14 Art.5	19		
Ch.17 by-laws 3,4			Yes
Ch.18 by-law 4	12		
Ch.22 by-law 2	17		
Ch.14 by-law 1	18,27		
By-law 3(b)	26		Art.5(a)

Reprinted from p.40 Human Rights Commission Occasional Paper No. 5.

BIBLIOGRAPHY

BOOKS

Bodley, John H (1972) 'Human zoos, living museums and real people' in *Victims of Progress*, Washington State University, Washington, Ch. 9.

Gale, Fay & Brookman, Alison (1972) *Urban Aborigines*. ANU Press, Canberra.

Maddock, Kenneth (1944) *The Australian Aborigines, a portrait of their society*. 2nd ed. Penguin Books, Ringwood, Vic.

Malezer, Les, Foley, Matt & Richards, Paul (1979) *Beyond the Act, Queensland Aborigines and Islanders, what do we want?* Foundation for Aboriginal and Islander Research Action, Brisbane.

Peterson, Nicolas (ed.) (1976) *Tribes and Boundaries in Australia*. Australian Institute of Aboriginal Studies, Canberra.

Roberts, J, Russell, B, Parsons, M (eds.) (1975) *The Mapoon Story by the Mapoon People*. Vol. 1 of 3 vols.

Rowley, Prof Charles D (1970) *The Destruction of Aboriginal Society*. Vol. 1, *Aboriginal policy and practice*. ANU Press, Canberra.

Tatz, Colin (1979) *Race Politics in Australia: Aborigines Po litics and Law*. University of New England Publishing Unit, Armidale, NSW.

World Council of Churches Programme to Combat Racism (1983) *Land Rights for Indigenous people.* WCC PCR publication 1983/no.16.

BOOKLETS, REPORTS & PAPERS

Aboriginal Advisory Council, 14th Meeting, Brisbane 4–5 August 1981, *Minutes.*

Aboriginal Advisory Council, 15th Meeting, Bamaga 6–8 July 1982, *Minutes.*

Aboriginal Advisory Council Working Party, Palm Island Meeting, 25–27 August 1982, *Minutes.*

Aboriginal Advisory Council Working Party, Cherbourg Meeting, 22–23 August 1982, *Minutes.*

Aboriginal Advisory Council Working Party, Brisbane Meeting, 2 December 1982, *Minutes.*

Aboriginal Advisory Council Working Party Meeting with Other Councillors and DAIA, Weipa Meeting, 25 October 1983, *Minutes.*

Aboriginal Development Commission (1983) *Aboriginal Housing and Accommodation Needs Survey.* Canberra.

Anderson, Christopher (1980) 'Multiple enterprise: contemporary Aboriginal subsistence strategy in Southeast Cape York Peninsula' in Stevens, N.C. & Bailey, A. (eds.) *Contemporary Cape York Peninsula.* The Royal Society of Queensland, Brisbane.

Australia, Department of Aboriginal Affairs (1984) Commonwealth paper tabled at QEF Area Advisory Committee Meeting, Cairns *Country Reserves - DOGIT*. Feb 1984.

Australia, Human Rights Commission (1983) 'Aboriginal reserves by-laws and human rights' (Occasional paper no.5). AGPS, Canberra.

Australia, Human Rights Commission (1983) 'Payment of award wages on Aboriginal reserves in Queensland' (Discussion paper no. 2). AGPS, Canberra.

Brennan, Frank SJ (1982) *Consultation documents on services legislation for Aborigines and Torres Strait Islanders in Queensland*. Queensland Catholic Bishops, Brisbane.

Brennan, Frank, SJ (1983) 'A comparison of Deeds of Grant in Trust (Amended) with Aboriginal Land Rights (N.T.) Act 1976' (Consultation document No.6, 19 December 1983). Unpublished, held by Queensland Catholic Bishops.

Brennan, Frank, SJ (1984) 'An analysis of the Community Services Bills' (Consultation document No.8, 12 April 1984). Unpublished, held by Queensland Catholic Bishops.

Brennan, Frank, SJ (1984) 'Land rights and self-determination for Queensland Aboriginal communities—what's been happening?' (Consultation document No.7, 3 January 1984). Unpublished, held by Queensland Catholic Bishops.

Brennan, Frank, SJ (1984) 'The new laws, Deed of Grant in Trust and services' (Consultation document No.9, 8 May 1984). Unpublished, held by Queensland Catholic Bishops.

Chase, Athol (1980) 'Cultural continuity: land and resources among East Cape York Aborigines' in Stevens, N.C. & Bailey, A. (eds.) *Contemporary Cape York Peninsula*. The Royal Society of Queensland, Brisbane.

Commissioner for Community Relations. *Annual reports,* 1976- Australian Government Publishing Service, Canberra.

Council, activities and directions 1982. Cairns, 1982.

Craig, Daniel (1979) *The social impact of the State on an Aboriginal reserve in Queensland, Australia.* PhD Thesis. University of California, Berkeley.

Human Rights Newsletter, no.7, Dec. 1983. Canberra, Human Rights Commission.

Hume, Lynne (1989) *Yarrabah: Christian Phoenix, Christianity and Social Change on an Australian Aboriginal Reserve.* PhD Thesis.

Law Reform Commission (1982) 'Aboriginal customary law - marriage children and the distribution of property' (Discussion paper no.18). Canberra.

Loos, Dr Noel (1976) *Aboriginal-European relations in North Queensland 1861-1897.* PhD Thesis. James Cook University, Townsville.

McIntyre, Greg (1984) 'Community services legislation.' Cairns. May 1984. Unpublished.

McIntyre Greg (1984) 'Do the Deeds of Grant in Trust and Community Services (Aborigines) Act achieve the fundamental goals of land rights?' Cairns. May 1984. Unpublished.

McIntyre, Greg (1984) 'Queensland land rights report, Deeds of Grant in Trust, an update. 8/6/83'. Cairns. Unpublished.

Miller, Barbara (1994) 'Options for the Future, Local Government and Native Title on Queensland Aboriginal Communities.' Aboriginal Coordinating Council.

Morse, Prof Brad (1983) 'Aboriginal land rights in Australia: a brief overview.' Aboriginal Development Commission, Canberra.

National Aboriginal Conference Secretariat Palm Island Workshop Brisbane, 8–11 May 1984. *Report.*

Nettheim, Prof Garth (1981) 'Possibilities for Commonwealth action' in Olbrei, Erik (ed.), *Black Australians: the prospects for change.* James Cook University Union, Townsville.

Nettheim, Prof Garth (1981) 'The Queensland Acts and human rights' in Olbrei, Erik (ed.), *Black Australians: the prospects for change.* James Cook University Union, Townsville.

Nettheim, Prof Garth (1984) *Community Services (Torres Strait) Bill 1984 and Community Services (Aborigines) Bill 1984.* Faculty of Law, University of NSW, Sydney.

Queensland, Department of Aboriginal and Islander Advancement. *Work in progress of Aboriginal Advisory Council Working Party, Report,* 19 July 1983.

Return to Country, The Homelands Movement in Australia, House of Representative Standing Committee on Aboriginal Affairs, March 1987.

Yarrabah Shire Council *Annual Report 2004–5*
http://yarrabah.qld.gov.au/wp-content/uploads/2015/04/Annual-Report-2004-05-Part-One.pdf

NEWSPAPERS AND ARTICLES

'Aurukun Marks Land Win.' *The Courier-Mail,* 10 November 1993, 14. John Koowarta is the 'Mabo of the Mainland.'

Carter, Jeremy Story (2015) 'Reboarding the Freedom Ride bus, 50 years on' 20 February 2015, http://www.abc.net.au/radionational/programs/rnafternoons/freedom-ride-50-years-on/6163446

Chesterman, John and Villafor, George (2000) 'Mr Neal's Invasion: Behind an Indigenous Rights Case', http://www.austlii.edu.au/au/journals/AUJlLawSoc/2000/1.pdf

Djunbunji Land and Sea Program News, http://www.djunbunji.com.au/news/yarrabah-title-determination/

Geiger, Dominic (2015) 'New Opportunities for Yarrabah after land transfer.' *The Cairns Post* 21/12/15, http://www.cairnspost.com.au/news/cairns/new-opportunities-for-yarrabah-after-land-transfer/news-story/

Gunn, Brian (1974) 'Yedinji Tribe Move Back to Buddabadoo.' *The Cairns Post* 30/9/1974.

http://www.crownlaw.qld.gov.au/resources/publications/queenslands-66th-native-title-win-for-indigenous-people

http://www.curtispitt.com.au/2011/12/19/combined-gunggandji-people%E2%80%99s-native-title-rights-recognised-at-yarrabah/

Keon-Cohen, B A (2000) 'The Mabo Litigation: A Personal and Procedural Account' *MelbULawRw* 35; (2000) 24(3) *Melbourne University Law Review* 893, http://www.austlii.edu.au/au/journals/MelbULawRw/2000/35.html

Korff, Jens (2016) 'Do We Have Apartheid in Australia?'
https://www.creativespirits.info/aboriginalculture/politics/do-we-have-apartheid-in-australia

'New Alliance in unity working for stronger Cape York
Communities' *Waanta Newsletter* of Lockhart River Sept 2013,
http://statements.qld.gov.au/Statement/Id/53104

Qld Government, 'Setting the Context',
http://www.qld.gov.au/web/community-engagement/guides-factsheets/atsi-communities/setting-context.html

'Queensland's Darkest Days' *The Guardian* 8 June 2005.

Vasis, Kimberly (2016) '7000 ha land returned to Yarrabah
traditional owners, the Gunggandji', *The Cairns Post* 18/6/16,
http://www.cairnspost.com.au/news/cairns/7000ha-land-returned-to-yarrabah-traditional-owners-the-gunggandji/news-story/

Warren Entsch presents the Boomerang Petition to Parliament on
behalf of Indigenous leader Norman Miller,
http://www.warrenentsch.com.au/Media/Speeches/tabid/74/articleType/ArticleView/articleId/996/Presenting-the-Boomerang-Petition-to-Parliament.aspx,
Miller Boomerang Petition http://youtu.be/a06cqhZfOwI

Yirrkala Bark Petitions (1963) (Cwth) *Documenting Democracy*,
http://www.foundingdocs.gov.au/item-did-104.html

QUEENSLAND PARLIAMENTARY PAPERS

Queensland Department of Native Affairs. *Annual Report 1963.* Pan.
Paper p.1061, Brisbane, 1963–64.

Queensland Legislative Assembly. *Hansard 1978*, vol.274.

Queensland Legislative Assembly. *Hansard* 1982, vol.289.

Queensland Legislative Assembly. *Hansard* 1983, vol.292.

Queensland Legislative Assembly. Hansard 1984, vol.294.

Queensland Parliament, Department of Aboriginal and Island Affair's. *Annual Report 1968.* Pan. Paper 1102. Brisbane, 1964.

ACTS OF PARLIAMENT QLD.

Aborigines Act 1971–1979

Aboriginal Land Act 1991 (Qld)

Amendment Act 1984

Community Services (Aborigines) Act 1984

Forestry Act 1959–1971

Land Act 1962–1983

Land Act (Aboriginal and Islander Land Grants)

Local Government Act 1936–1983

Local Government (Aboriginal Lands) Act 1978

Local Government (Community Government Areas) Act 2004 (Qld)

Native Title (Queensland) Act 1993 (Qld)

The Aborigines Regulations 1972

The Aboriginal Relics Preservation Act of 1967

Torres Strait Land Act 1991 (Qld)

ACTS OF PARLIAMENT COMMONWEALTH

Aboriginal and Torres Strait Islanders (Queensland Discriminatory Laws) Act 1975

Aboriginal and Torres Strait Islanders (Queensland Reserves and Communities Self-Management) Act 1978 Human Rights Commission Act 1981

Aboriginal Land Rights (Northern Territory) Act 1976 (Cth)

Native Title Act 1993 (Cth)

Native Title Amendment Act 1998 (Cth)

Northern Territory National Emergency Response Act 2007 (Cth)

Queensland Aboriginals and Torres Strait Islanders (Self-Management and Land Rights) Act 1981

Racial Discrimination Act 1975

INTERNATIONAL LAWS

UN General Assembly, *International Convention on the Elimination of All Forms of Racial Discrimination*, 21 December 1965, United Nations, Treaty Series, vol. 660, p. 195, available at: http://www.refworld.org/docid/3ae6b3940.html [accessed 20 September 2016]

UN General Assembly, *International Covenant on Civil and Political Rights*, 16 December 1966, United Nations, Treaty Series, vol. 999, p. 171, available at: http://www.refworld.org/docid/3ae6b3aa0.html [accessed 20 September 2016]

Books by the Author

Miller, B (2018) White Woman Black Heart: Journey Home to Old Mapoon, A Memoir, Createspace and Barbara Miller Books

Miller, B. (2016) The Dying Days of Segregation in Australia: Case Study Yarrabah. Updated 2nd edition 2018 by Barbara Miller Books.

Miller, B. (2014) The European Quest to Find Terra Australis Incognita: Quiros, Torres and Janszoon.

Miller, B. (2012) William Cooper, Gentle Warrior: Standing Up for Australian Aborigines and Persecuted Jews, Xlibris.

Miller, B. (2006) 'The Re-Founding of Australia' in Maeliau, M., Maki, J., Miller, B. and Siilata, M. Uluru: the Heart of Australia, Honiara, Solomon Is.

Miller, B. (1992) 'A Social-Historical and Psychological Perspective on Aboriginal Intra-Cultural Aggression' in Thomas, D. and Veno, A. (Eds) Psychology and Social Change, Creating an International Agenda, The Dunmore Press: Palmerston North, New Zealand.

Roberts, J.P., Russell, B., and Parsons, M., (1975) (Eds) The Mapoon Story by The Mapoon People, Volume 1, International Development Action: Fitzroy, Victoria and printed by Amber Press, Sydney.

Roberts, J.P., Parsons, M., and Russell, B. (1975) *The Mapoon Story According to the Invaders: Church Mission, Queensland Government and Mining Company*, Volume 2, International Development Action: Fitzroy, Victoria and printed by Amber Press, Sydney.

Free

I'd like to give you a free chapter from another book of mine. It tells you the untold story of the first Europeans to set foot on Australia. It was at Mapoon. Just use this link to download it.

http://eepurl.com/dn69ab

If you enjoyed my book, please go to Amazon and leave a few comments as a review and/or send me a few comments at bmiller-books@bigpond.com

And visit my facebook page - https://www.facebook.com/Barbara-Miller-Books-479991872149265/

Watch for my follow up books in my series - *Australian Aboriginal Issues Series*

My follow up memoir will also be titled *White Woman Black Heart* but will have a different subtitle and I hope to have it out in 2018.

Keep an eye out for a series of books I'm working on called *Faces of Eve* with stories of Jewish women Holocaust or Shoah Survivors and stories of Christian women from the Middle East who have faced persecution.

How did I learn to self-publish?

You can too!! Is there a book in you waiting to come out?
Find out how? What are the secrets of the trade?

Go to this link for a **free webinar** that shows you how

- The **3-Step System** I use to write, publish, and launch a book quickly that people will want to read and buy and how to use your book to leave a legacy.
- An approach to **find your book idea quickly instead of having writer's block** - and turn your idea into a finished book in just 3 steps, a book that could open doors to speaking engagements and business opportunities and more. Find your voice.

https://xe172.isrefer.com/go/sps4ftavts/bookbrosinc5886

Made in the USA
Las Vegas, NV
01 November 2021

33482704R00114